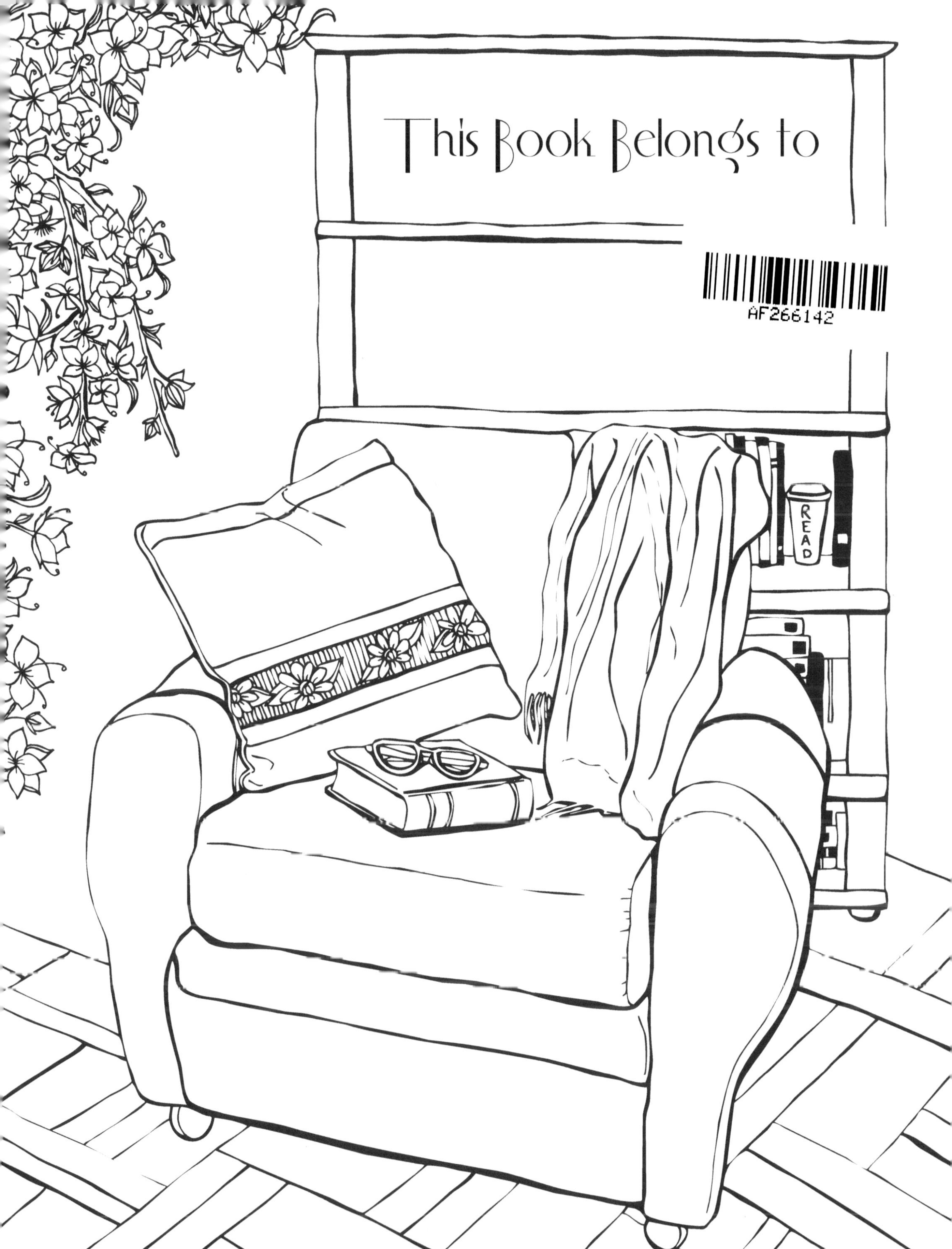

This Book Belongs to
READ
AF266142

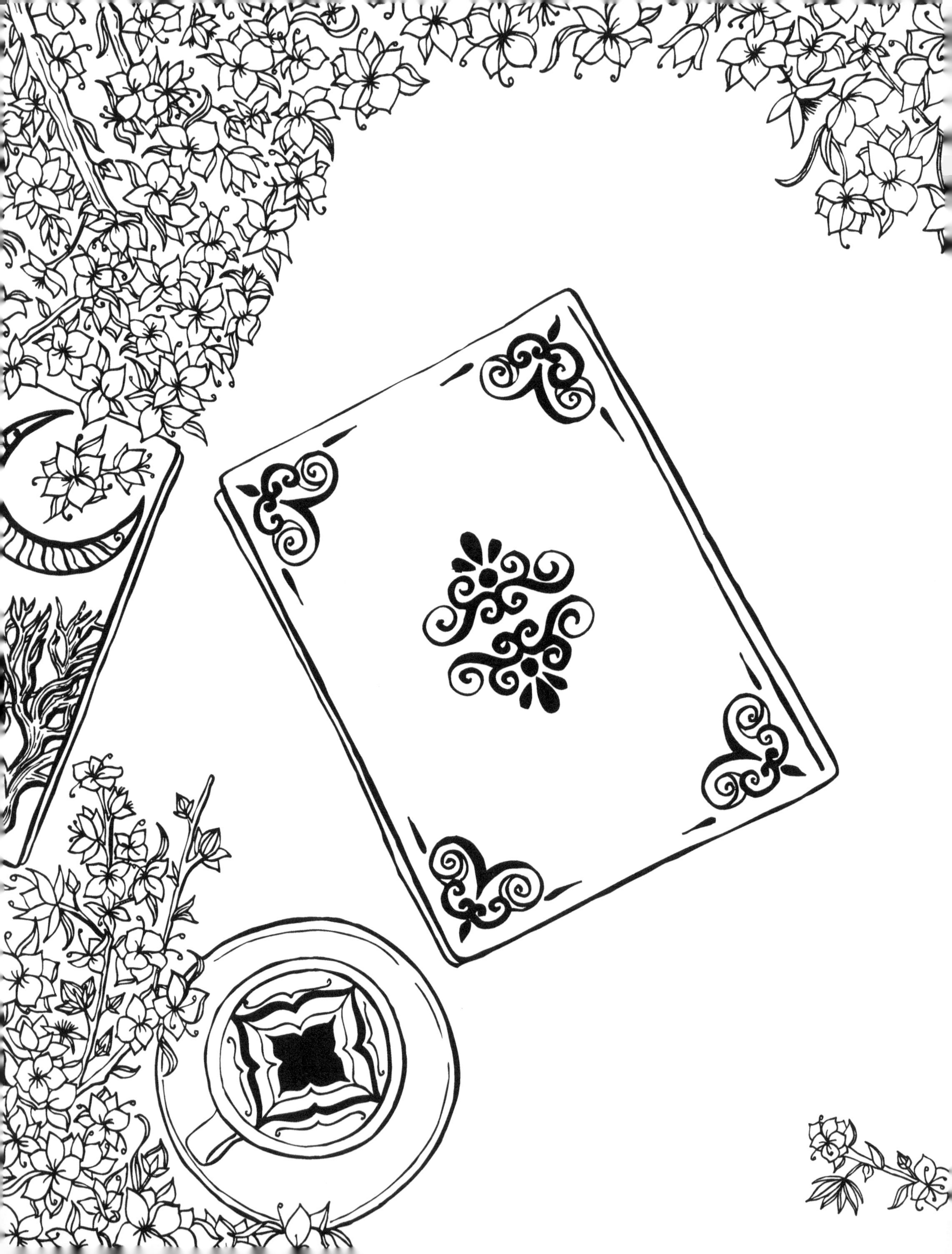

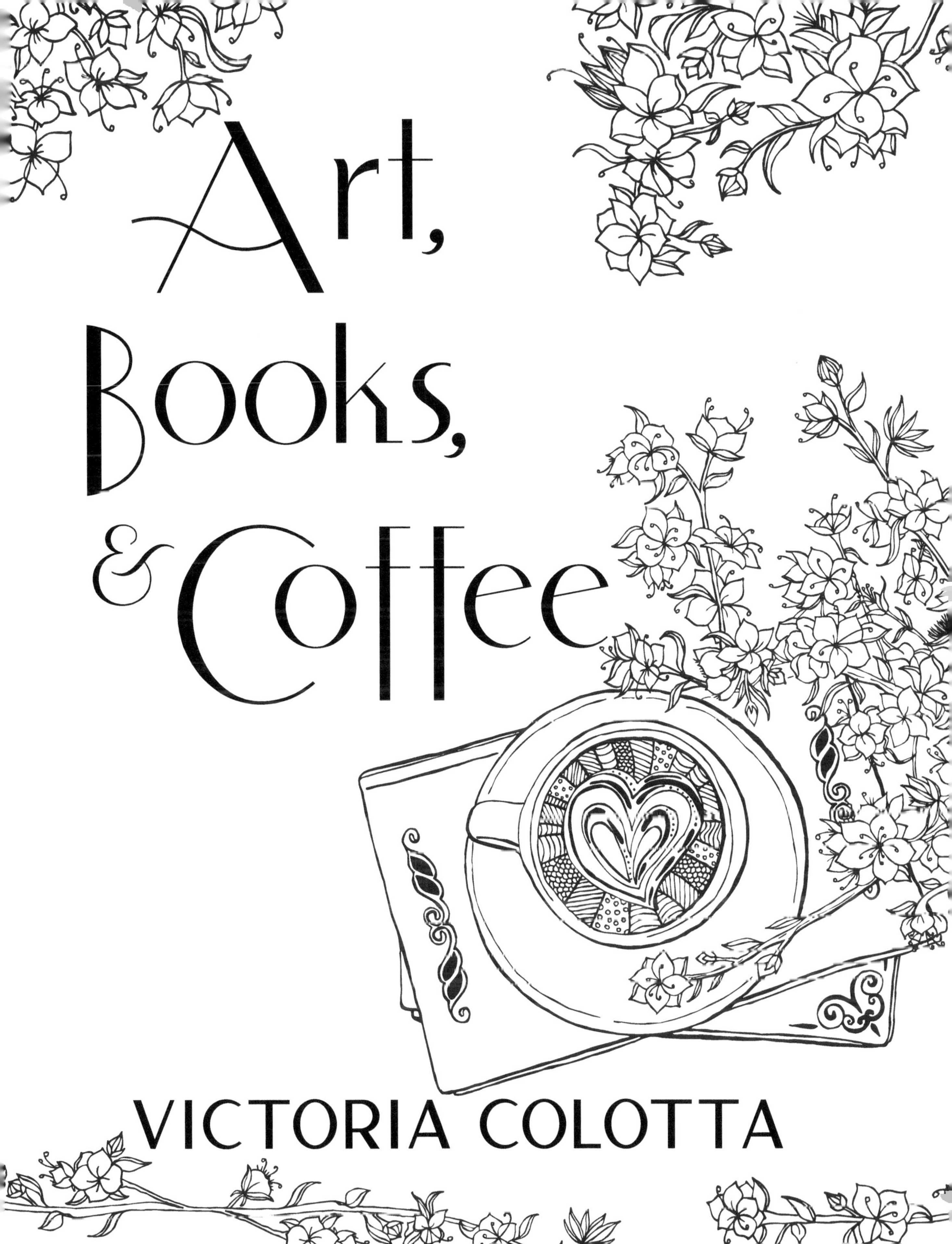

# Art, Books, & Coffee

## VICTORIA COLOTTA

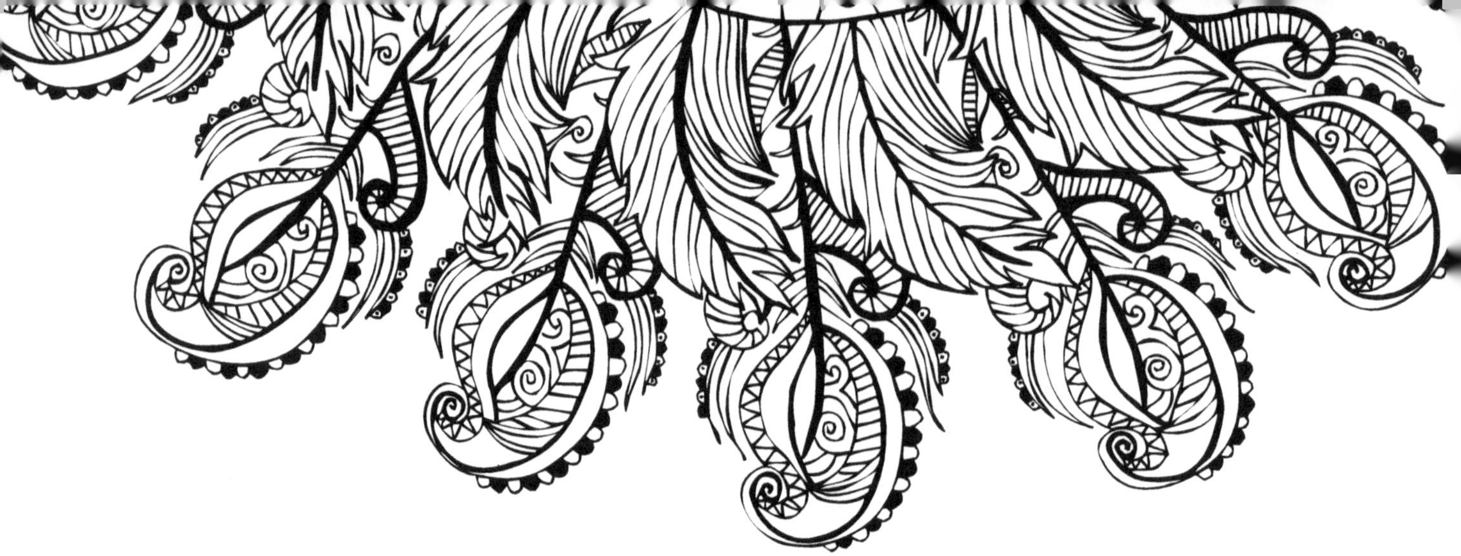

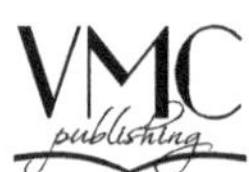

Published by VMC Publishing, a division of VMC Art & Design, LLC
P.O. Box 153, Allendale, NJ 07401
www.vmc-artdesign.com



ISBN: 978-0-9980771-3-0

Cover and Interior Design by VMC Art & Design, LLC

Printed in the United States of America

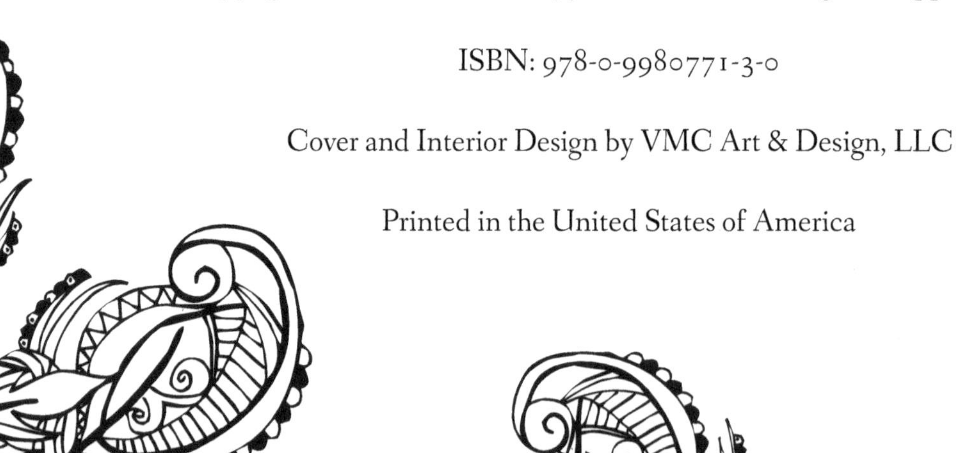

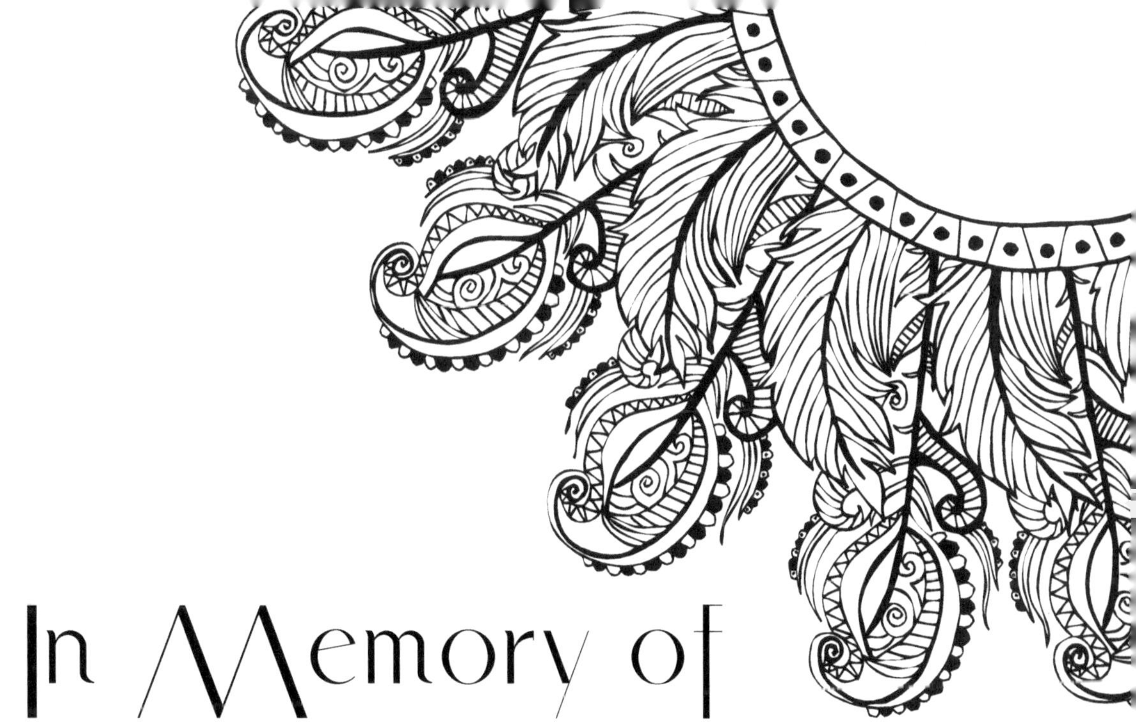

# In Memory of

My Uncle Jimmy, the best godfather a girl could ask for.

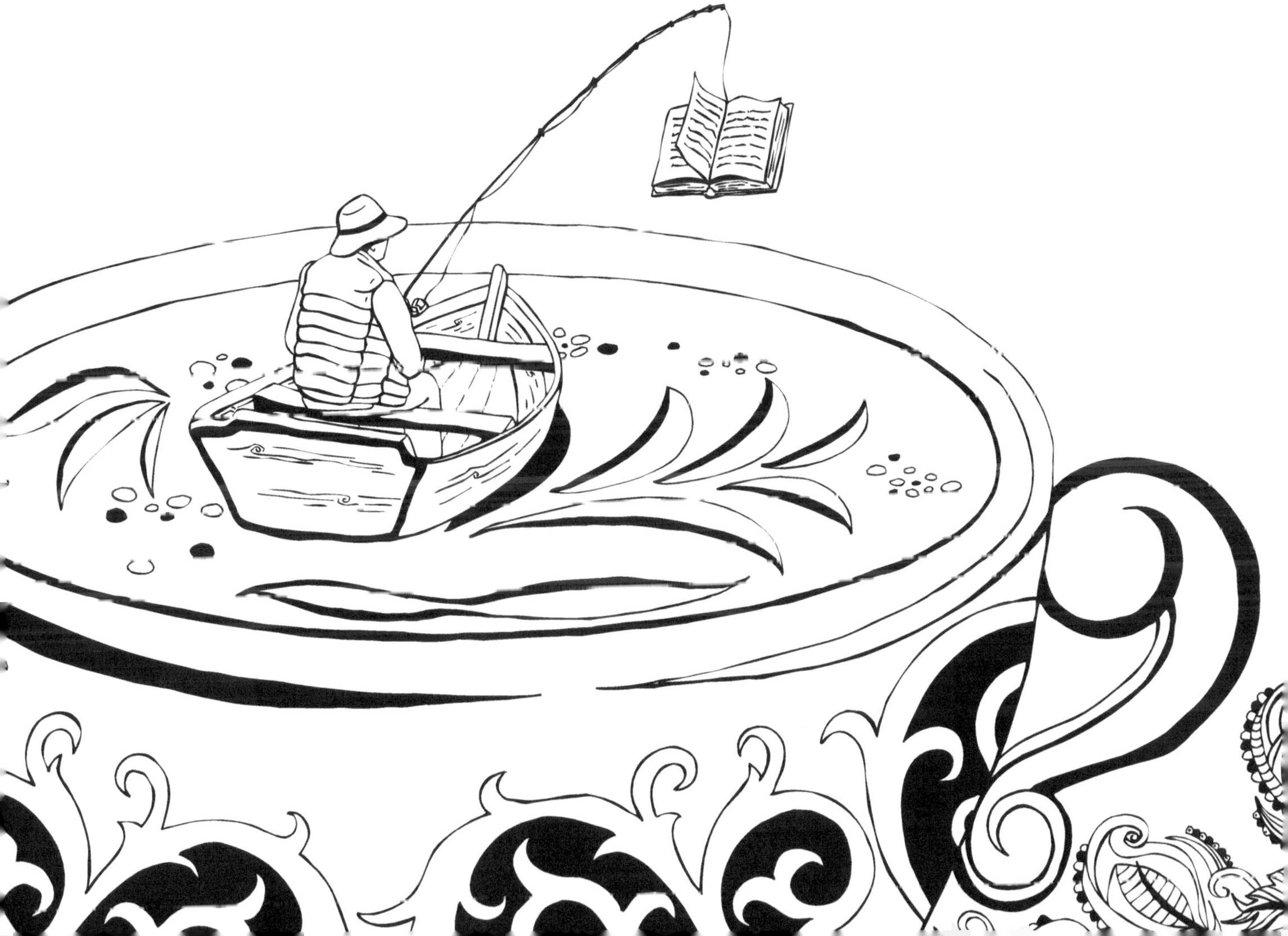

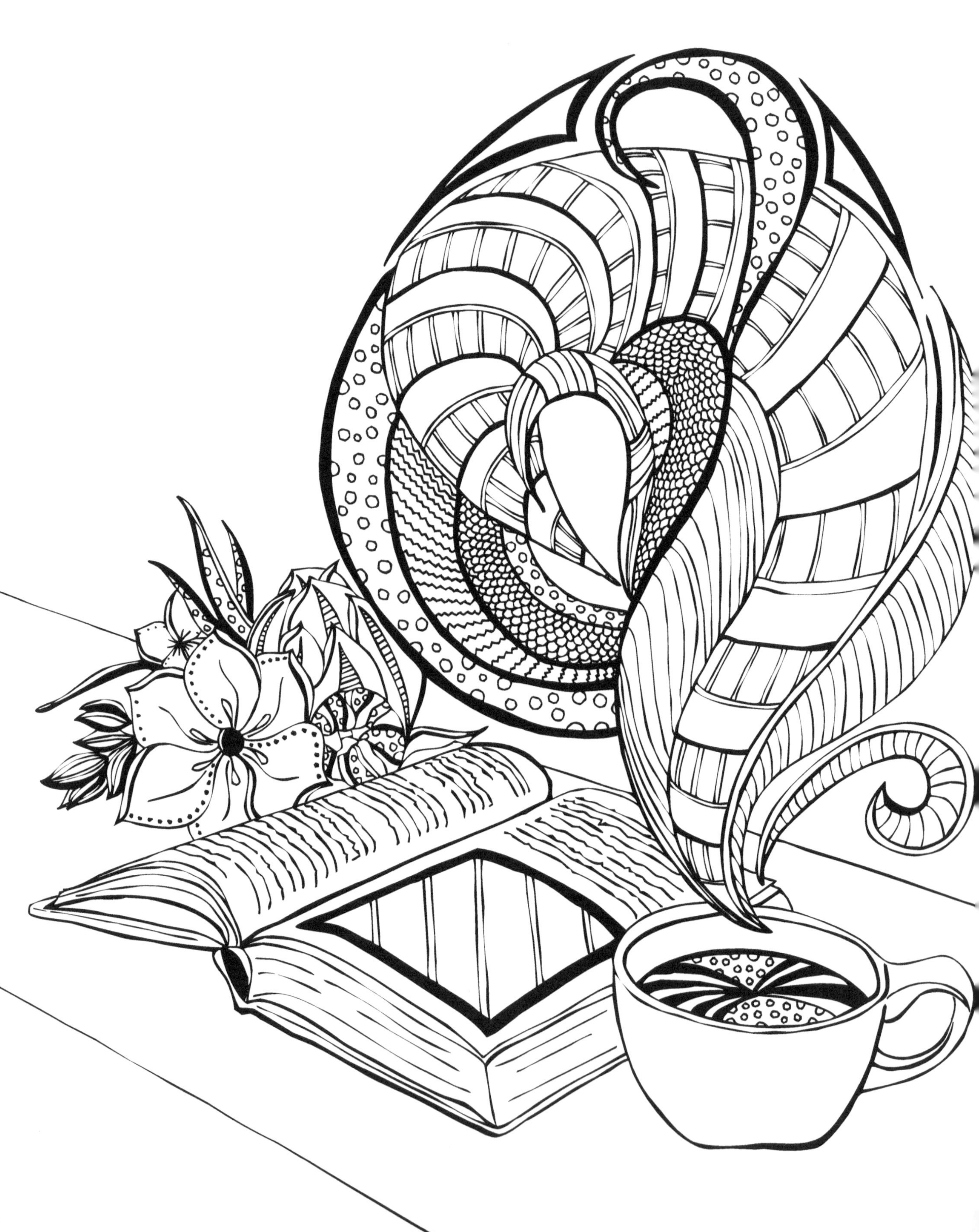

Inspired by the three passions in her life, artist, and author Victoria Colotta has created her first solo coloring book—ART, BOOKS, & COFFEE. It is a collection of carefully curated hand-drawn illustrations using the books of some of today's bestselling authors as well as photographs from the top bookstagrammers.

As you color your way through the book, you will be able to sit in a New York City cafe, enter into a fairyland, and enjoy some wonderfully bookish renderings. This coloring book is the perfect way to unwind in a world of art, books, and coffee.

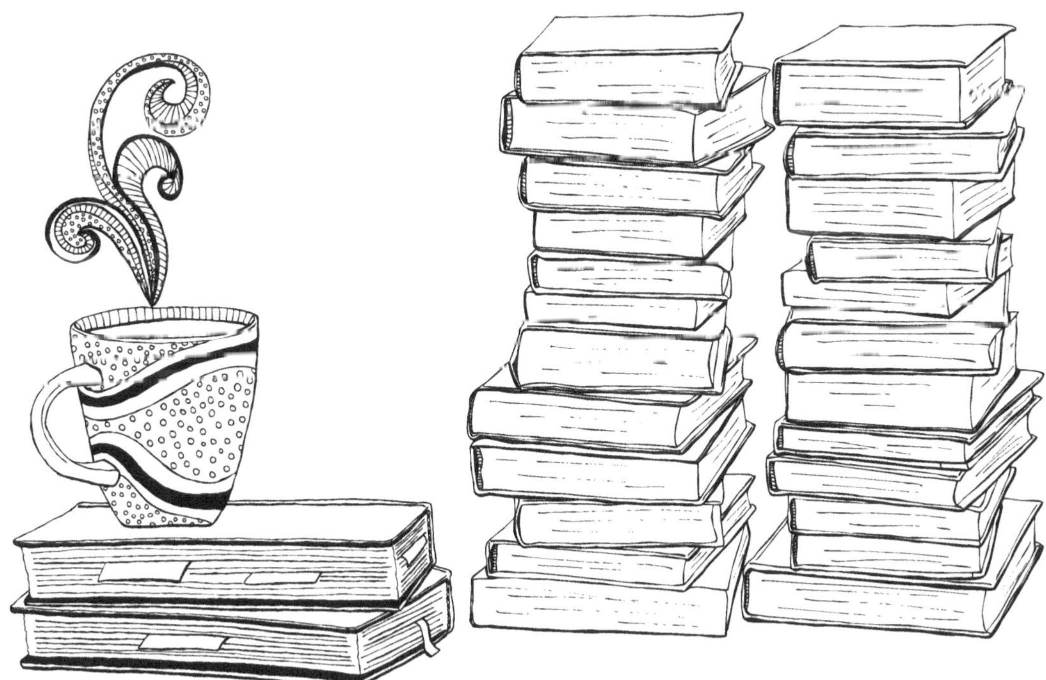

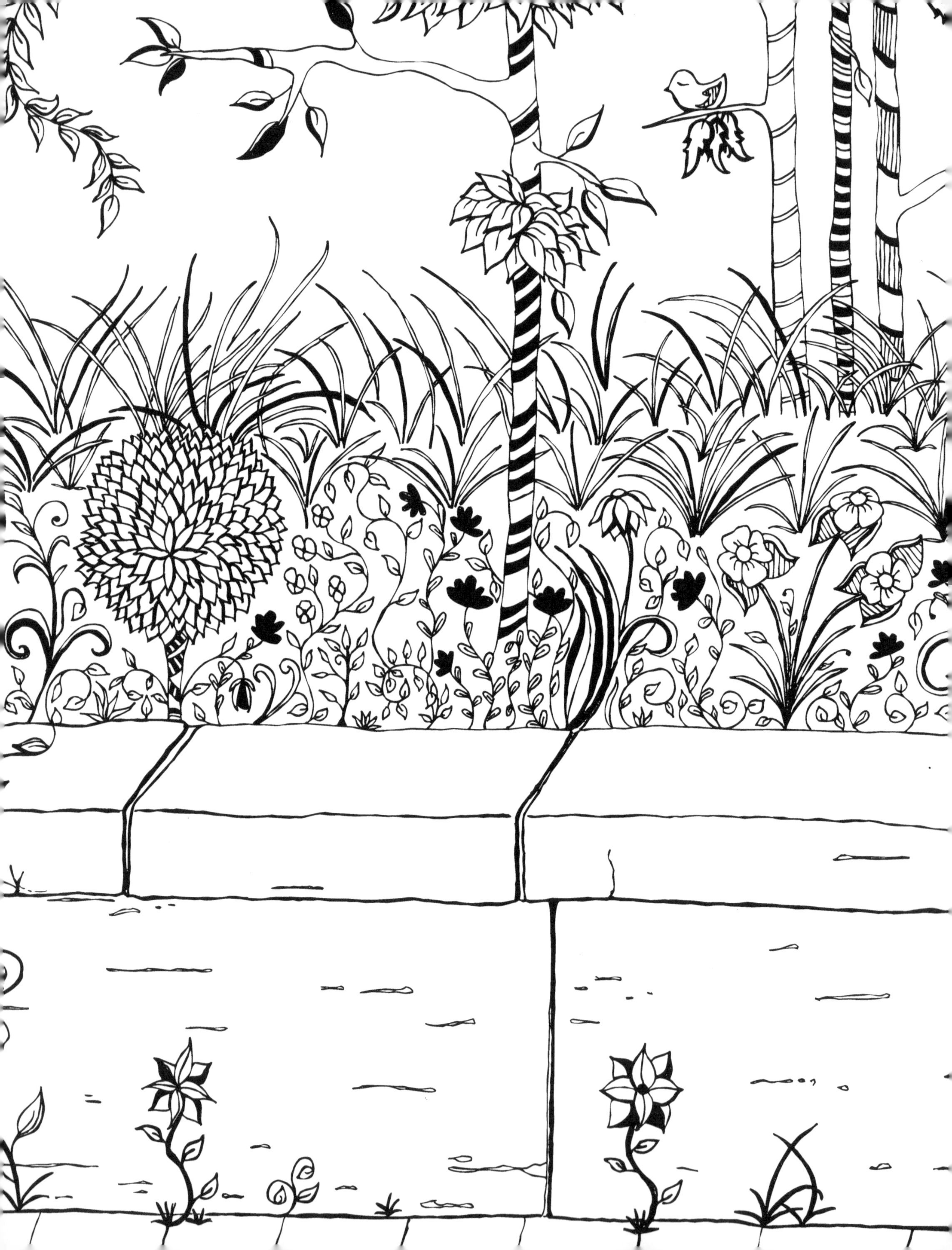

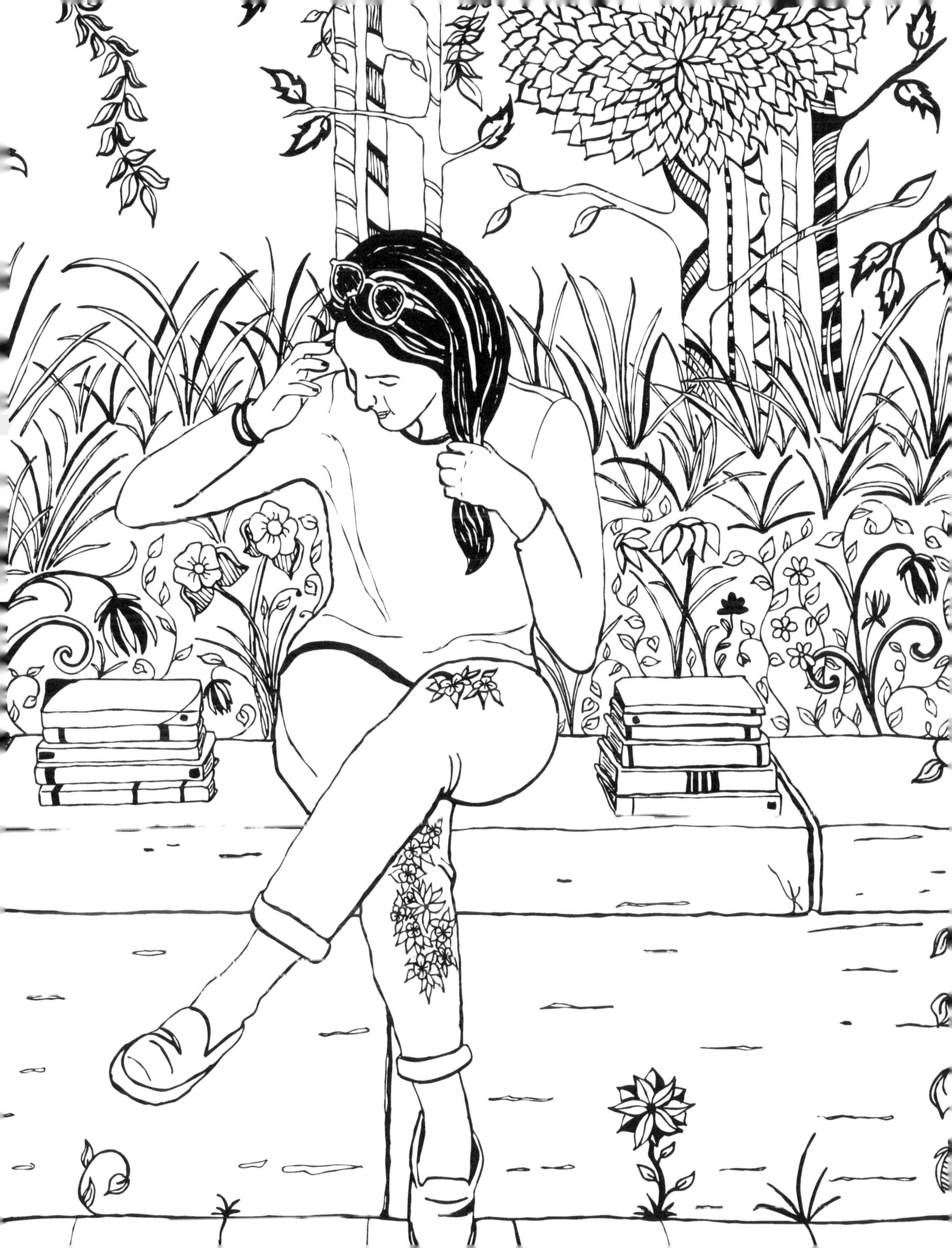

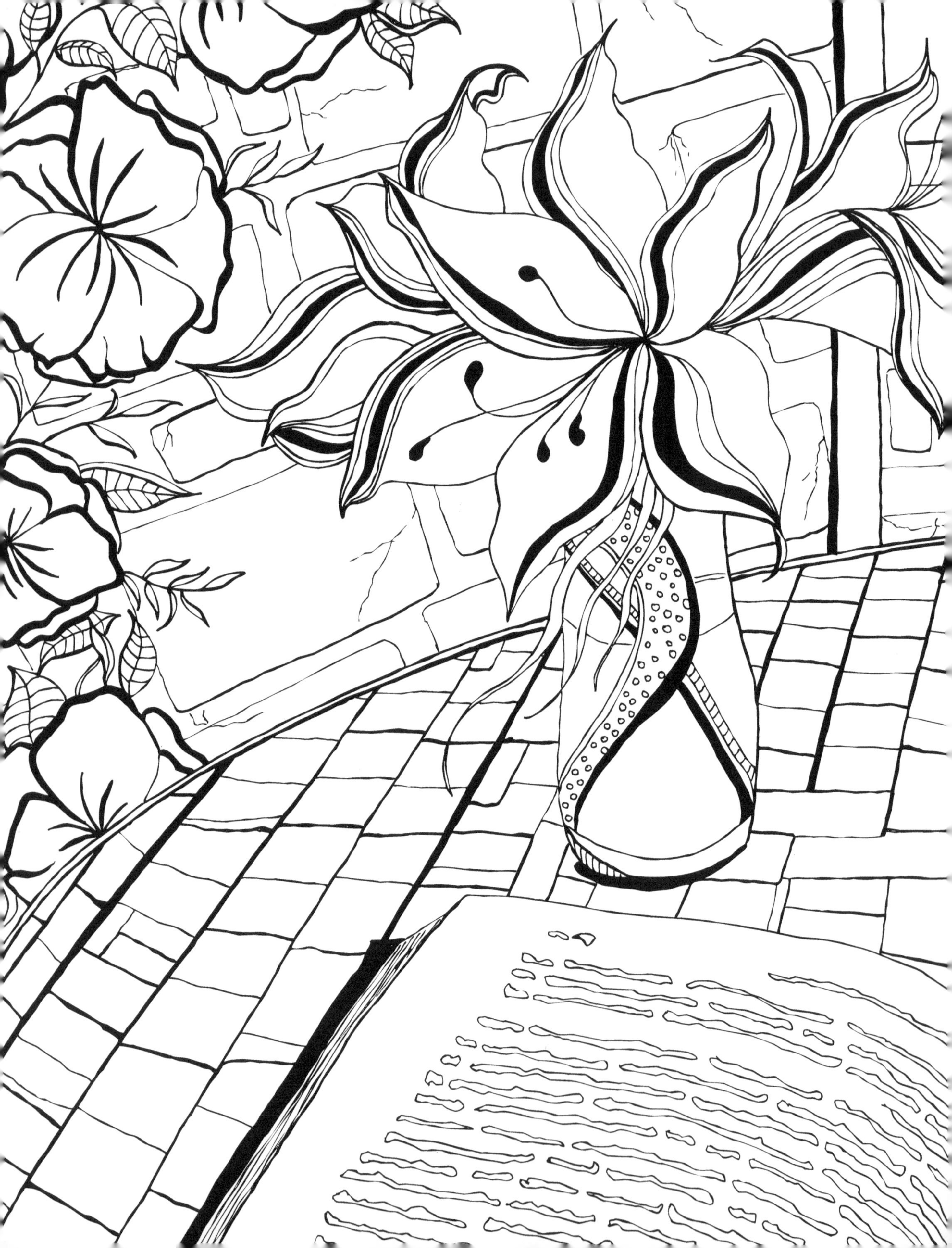

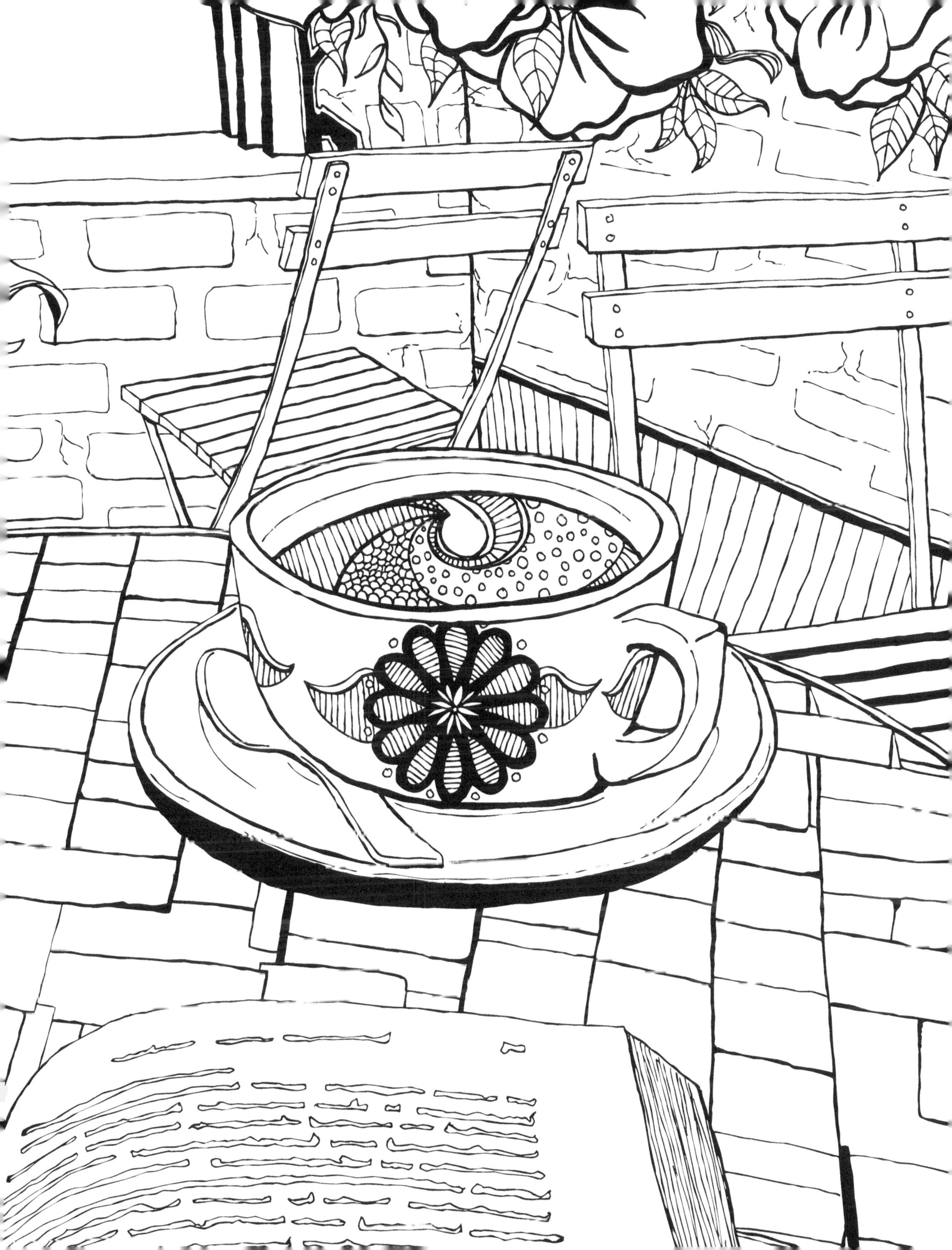

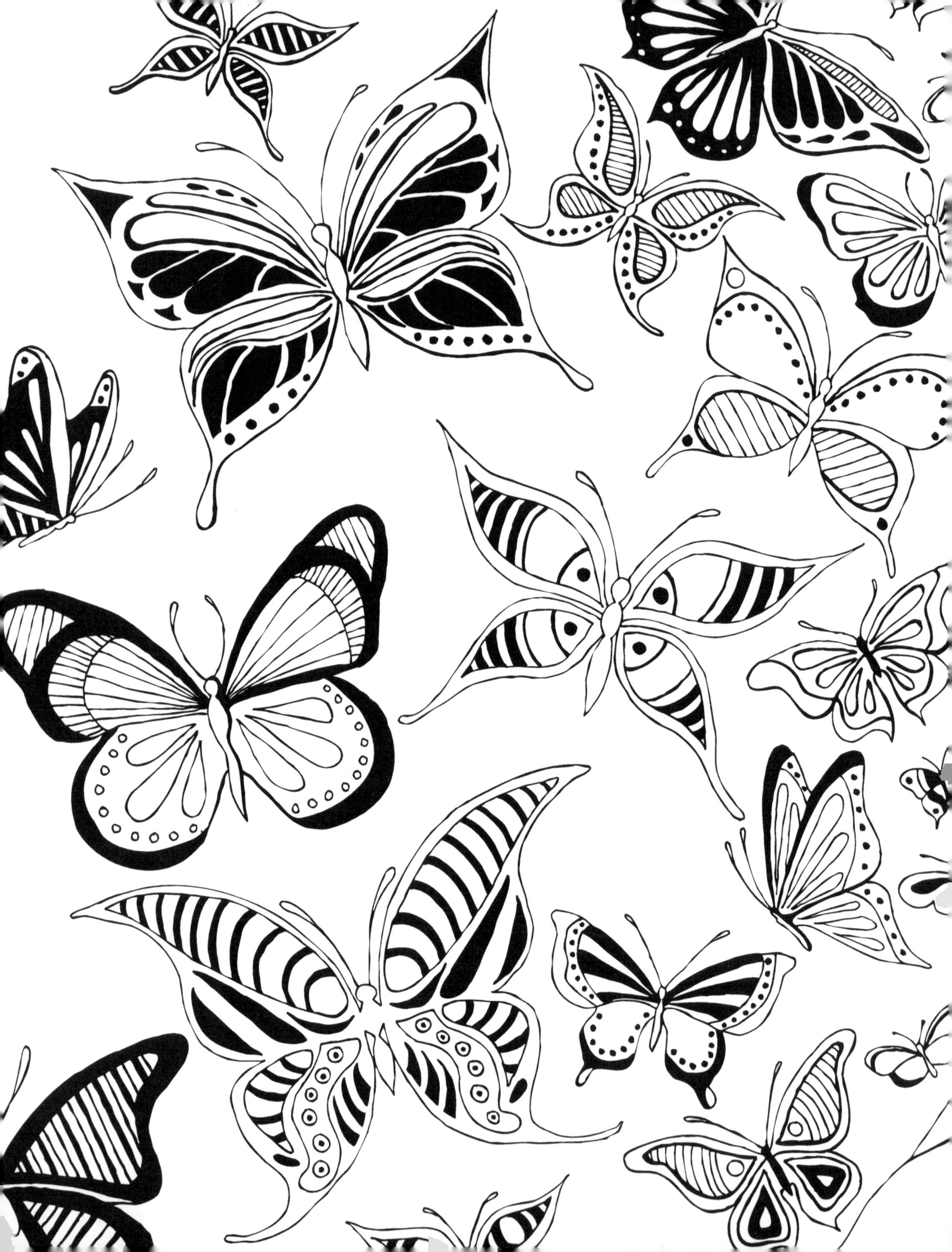

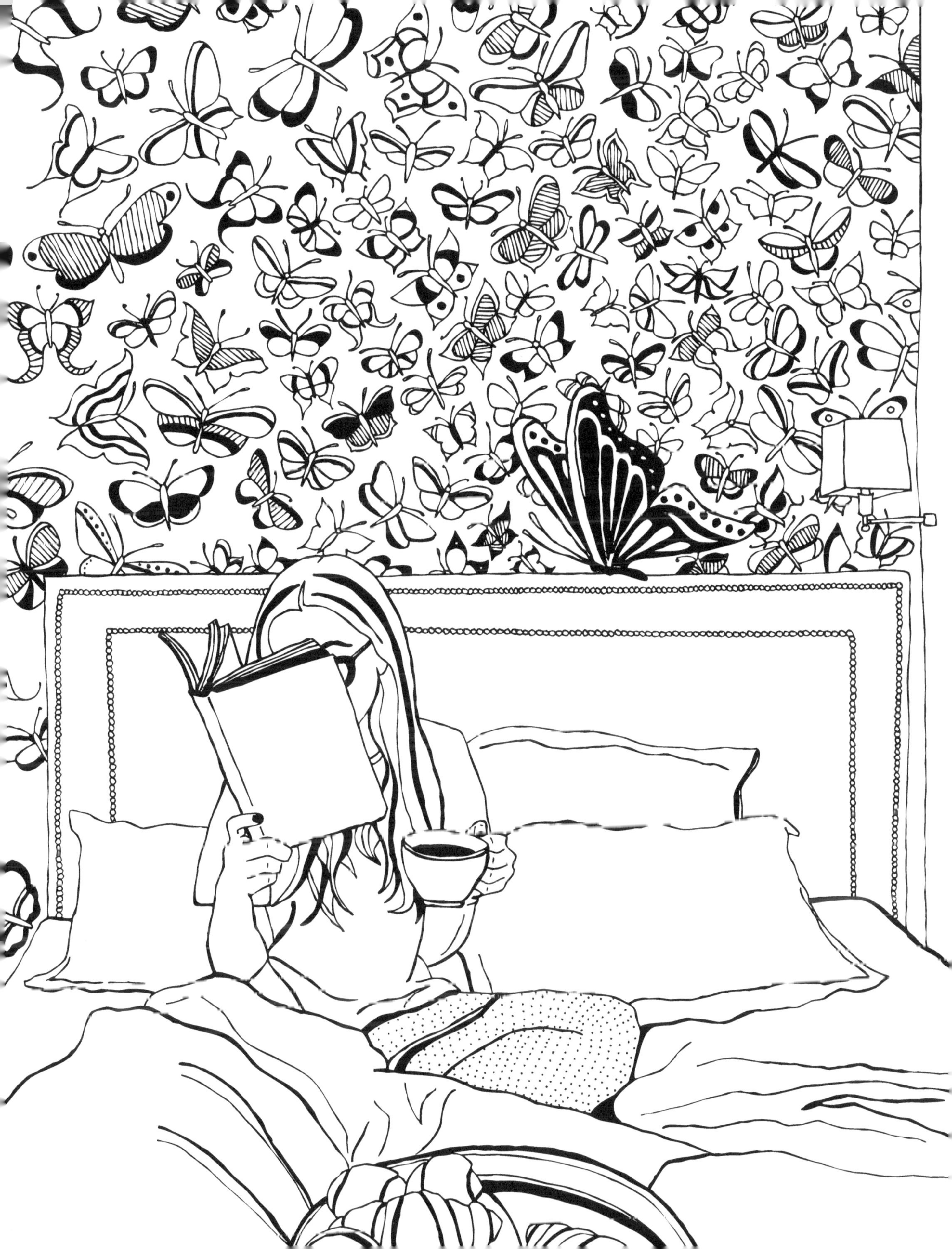

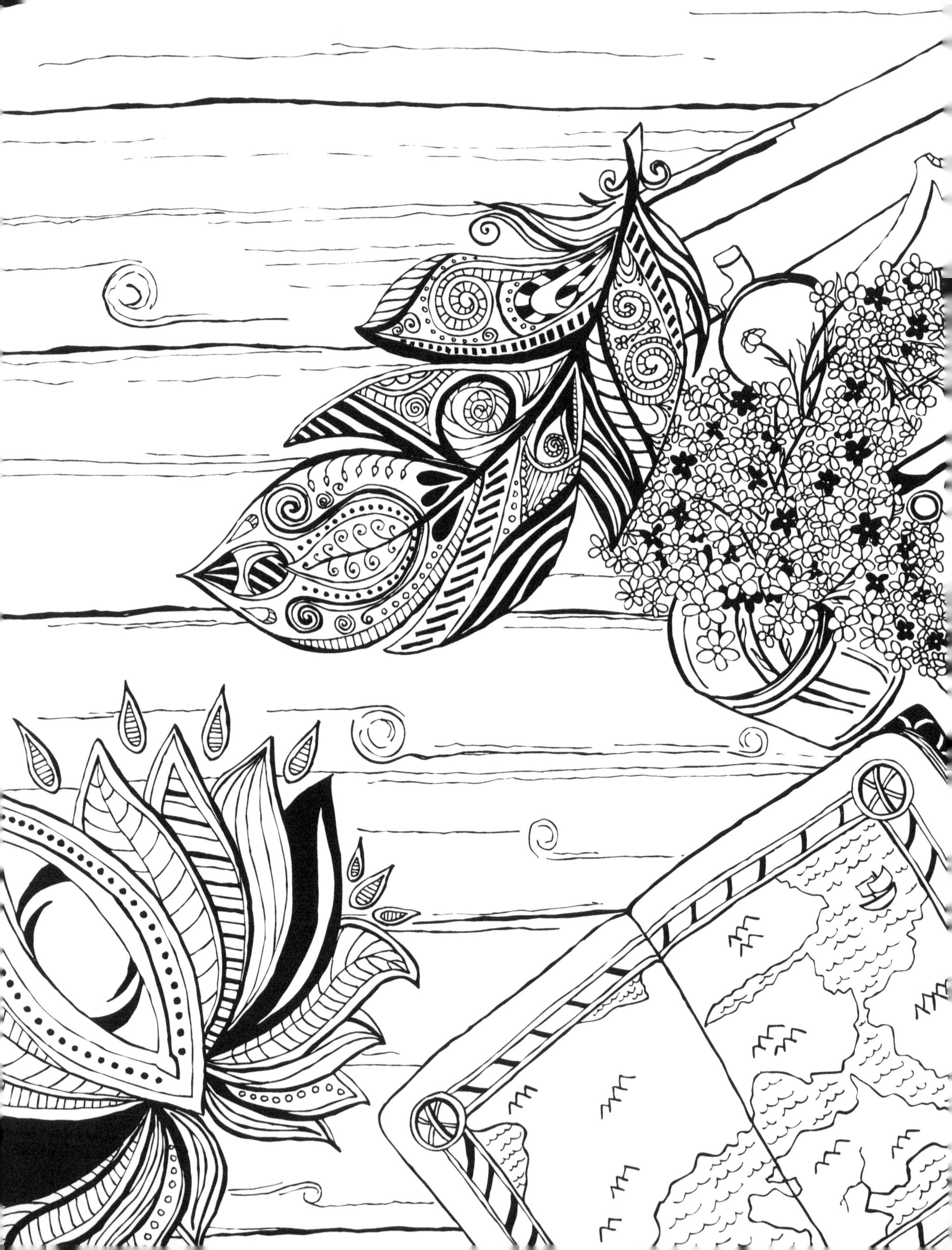

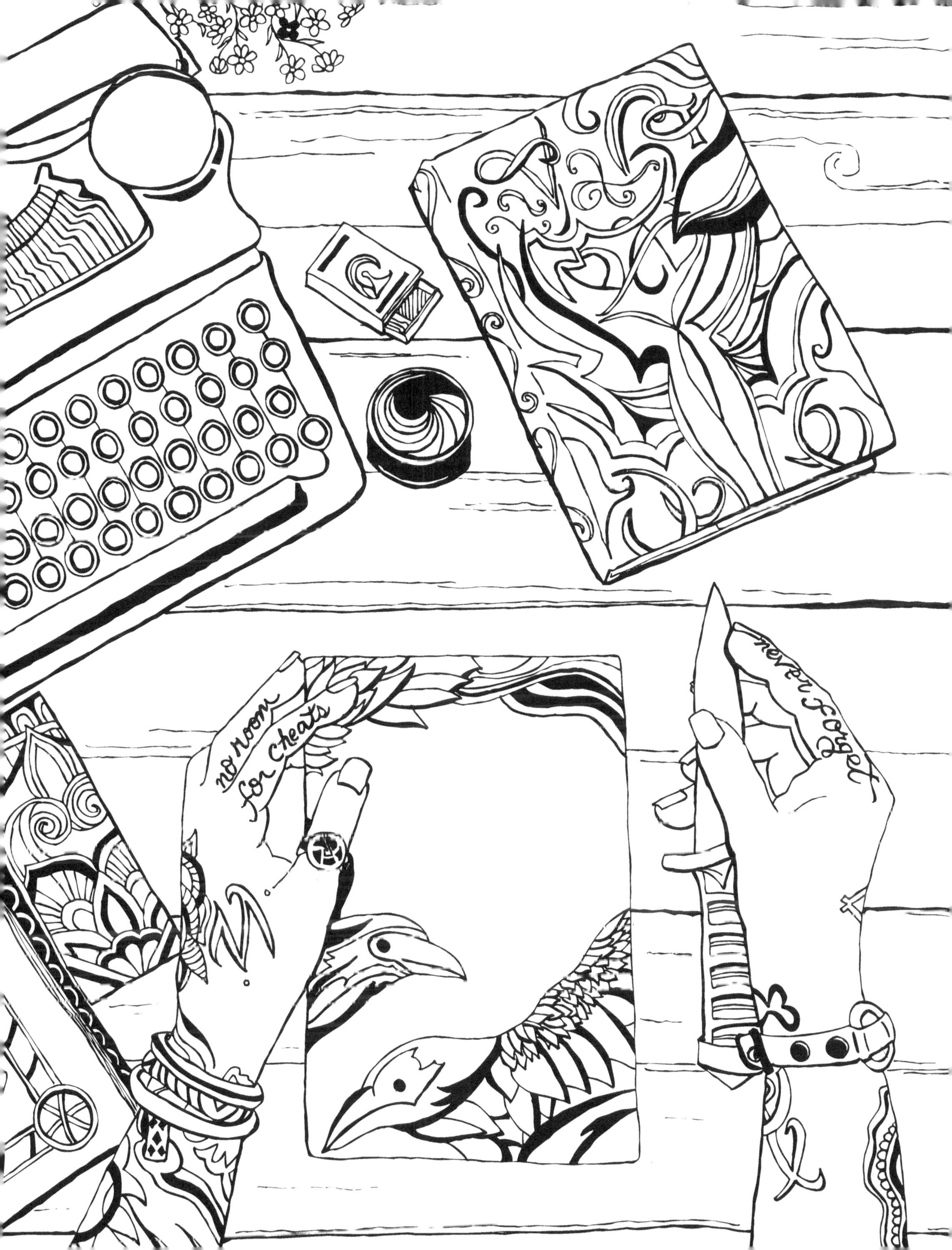
no room
for cheats
neveu forget

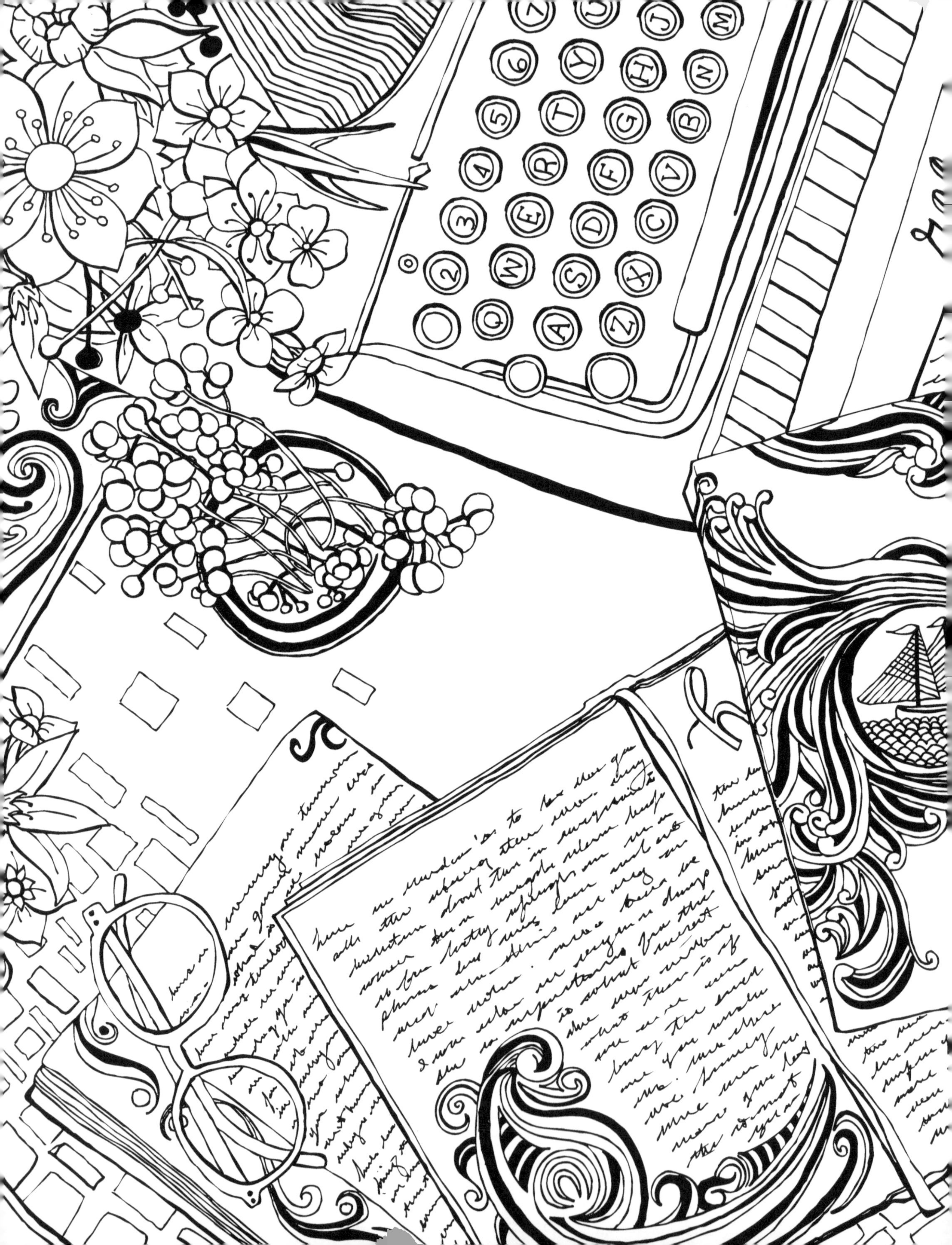

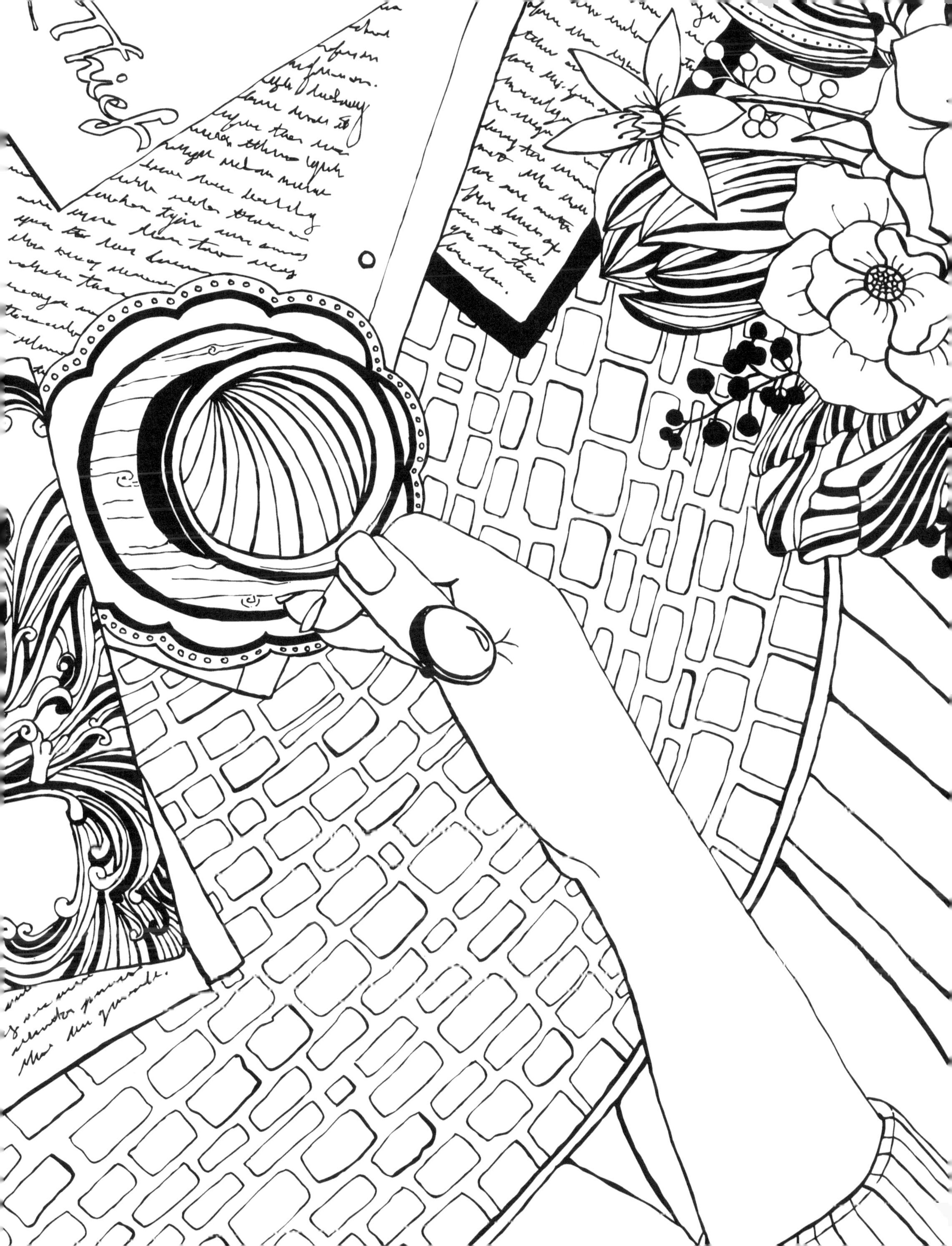

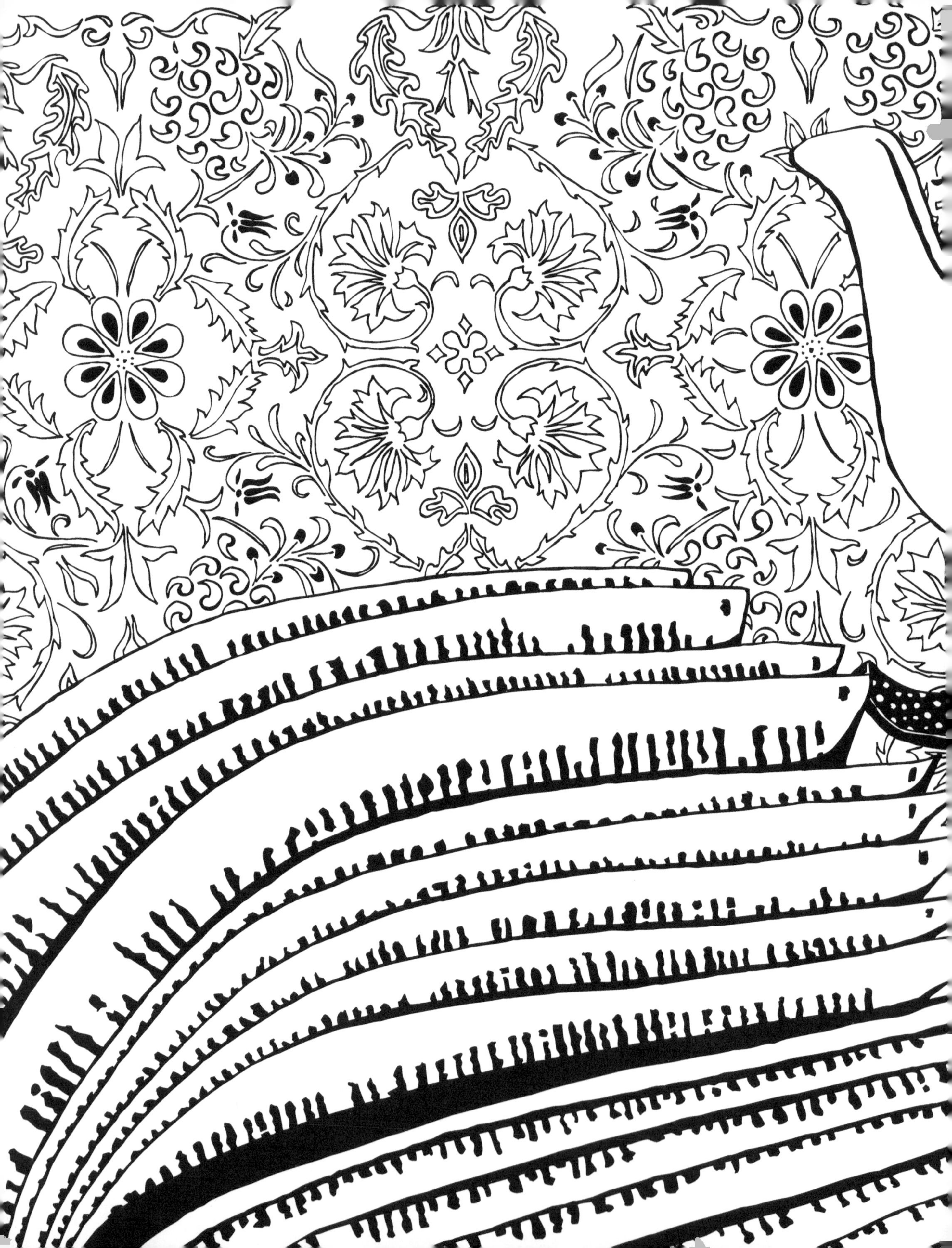

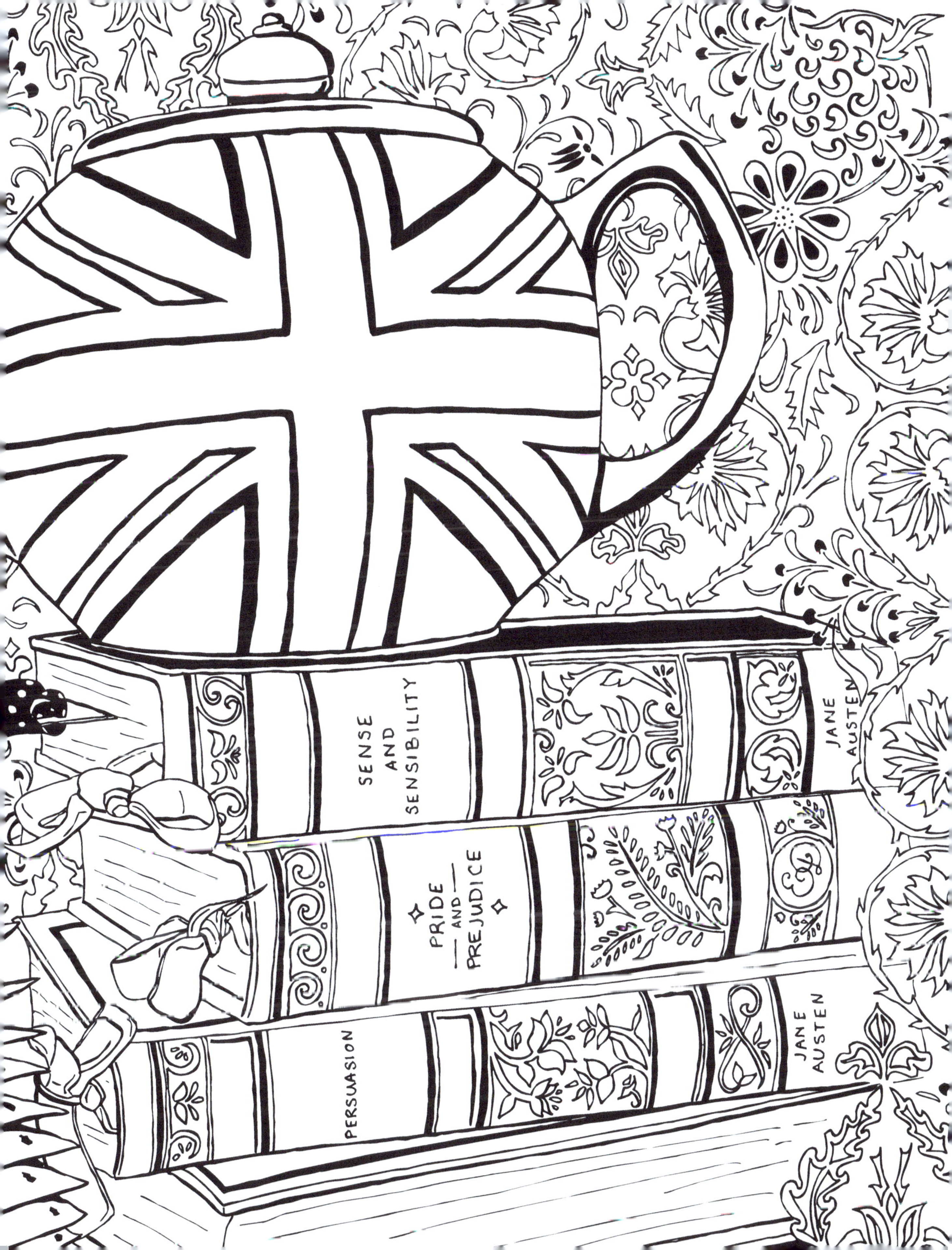

SENSE AND SENSIBILITY
JANE AUSTEN
PRIDE AND PREJUDICE
PERSUASION
JANE AUSTEN

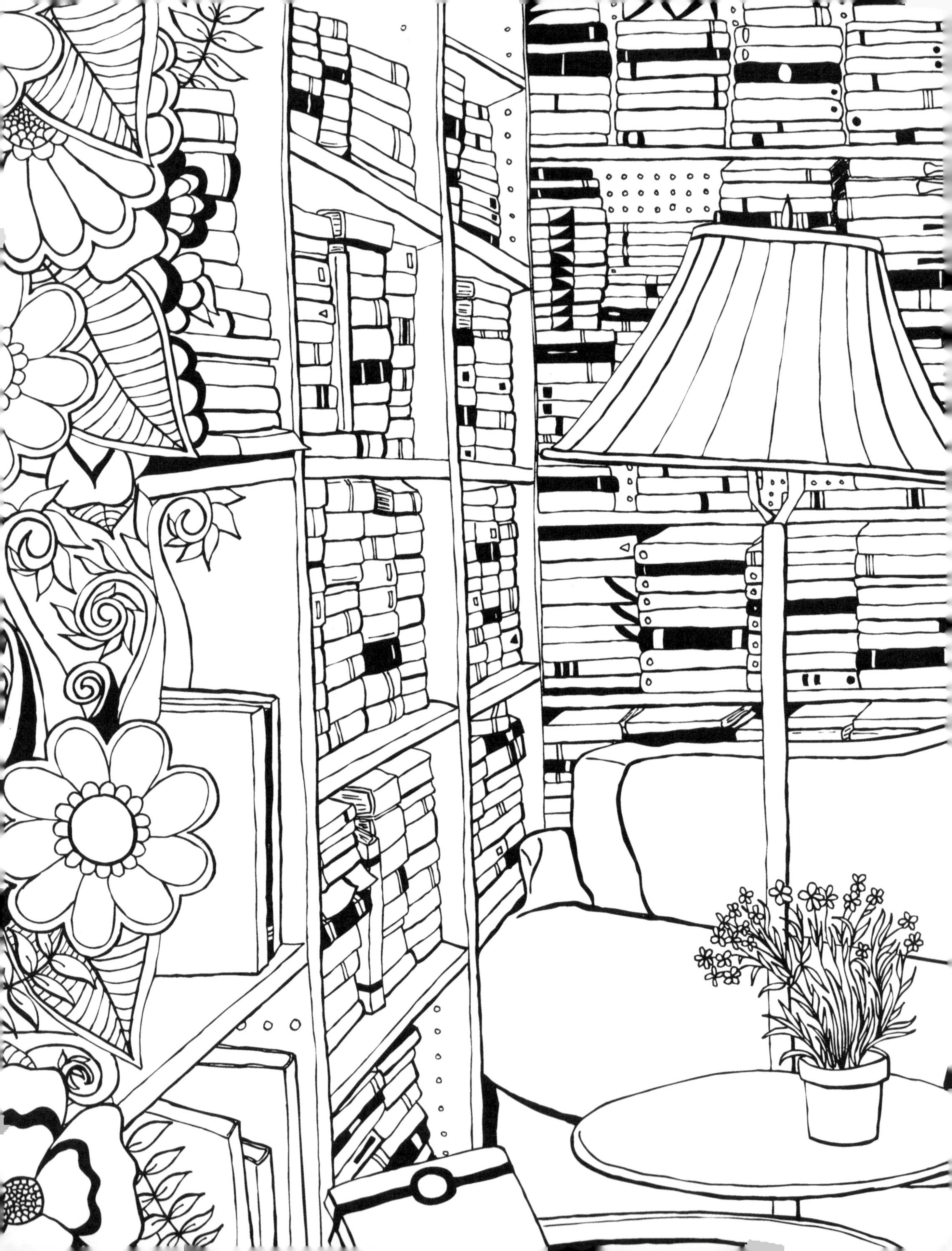

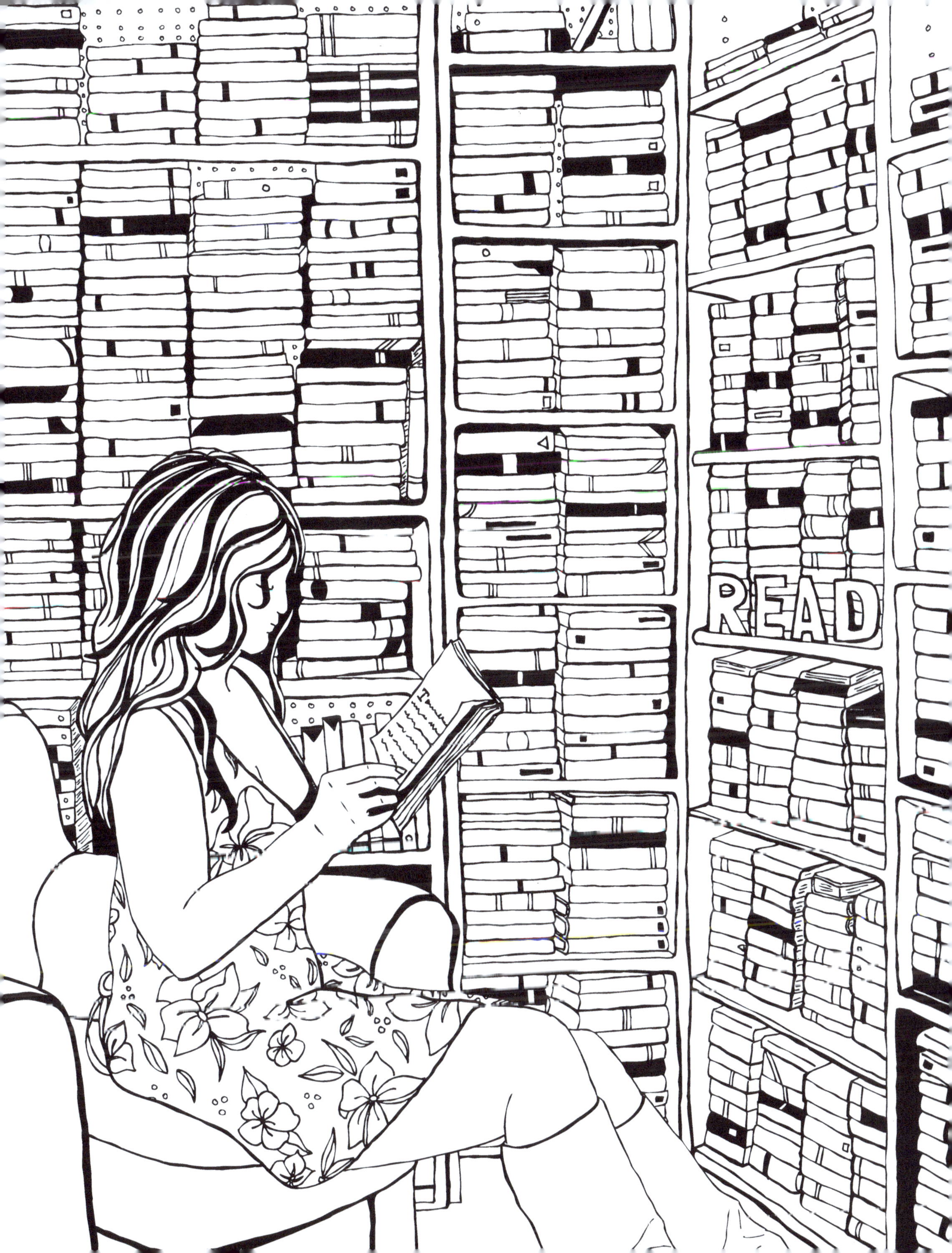

READ

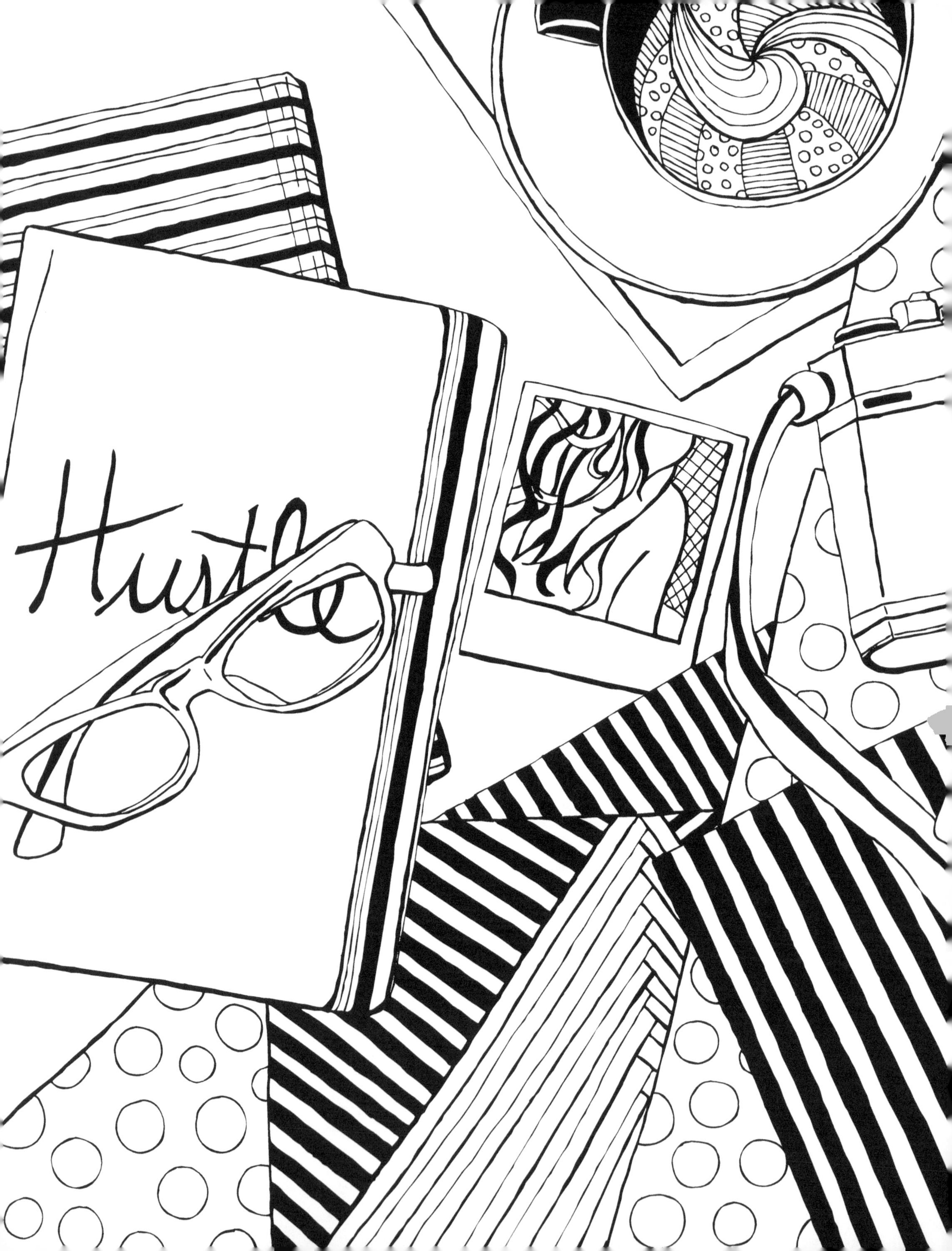
Hustle

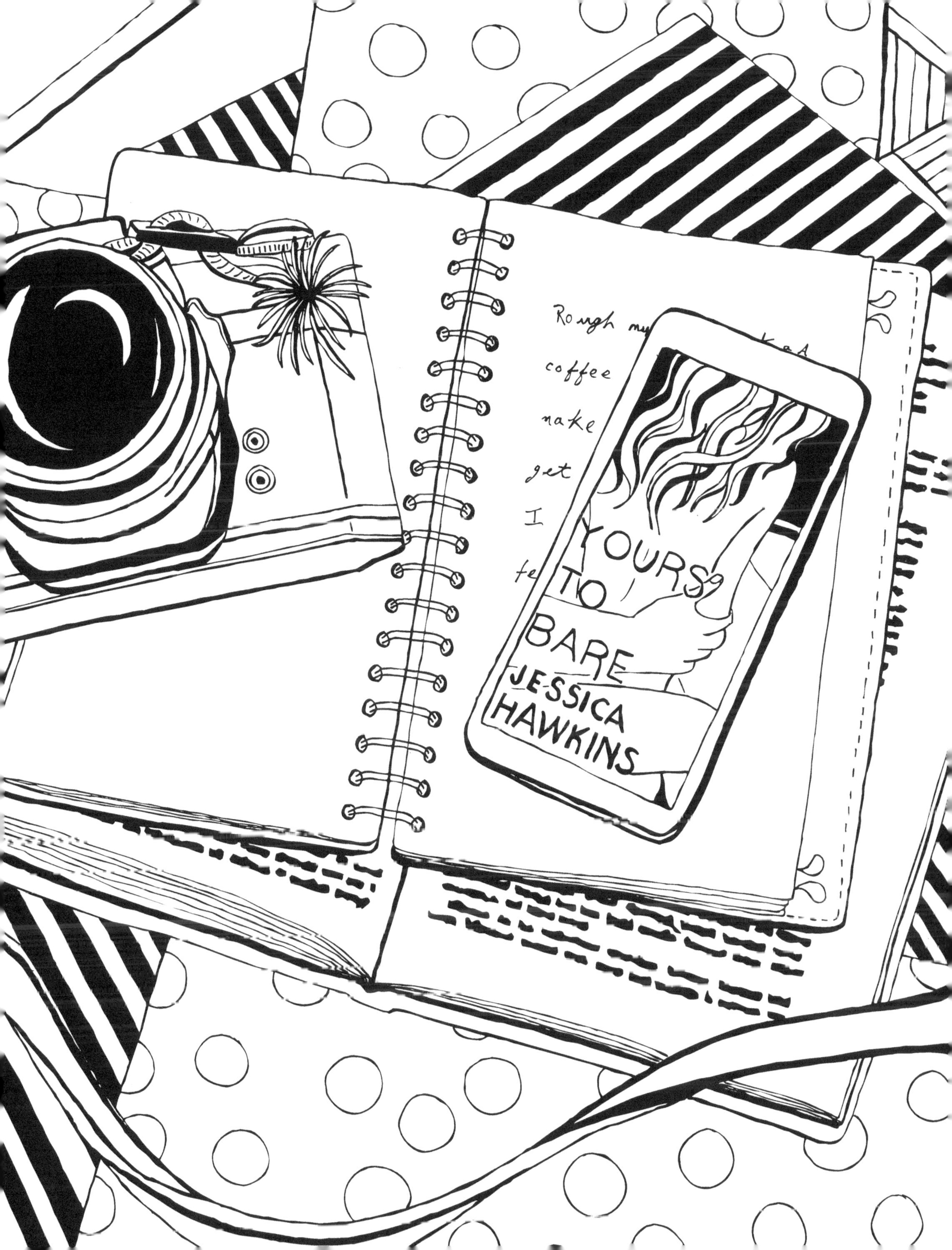
YOURS
TO
BARE
JESSICA
HAWKINS

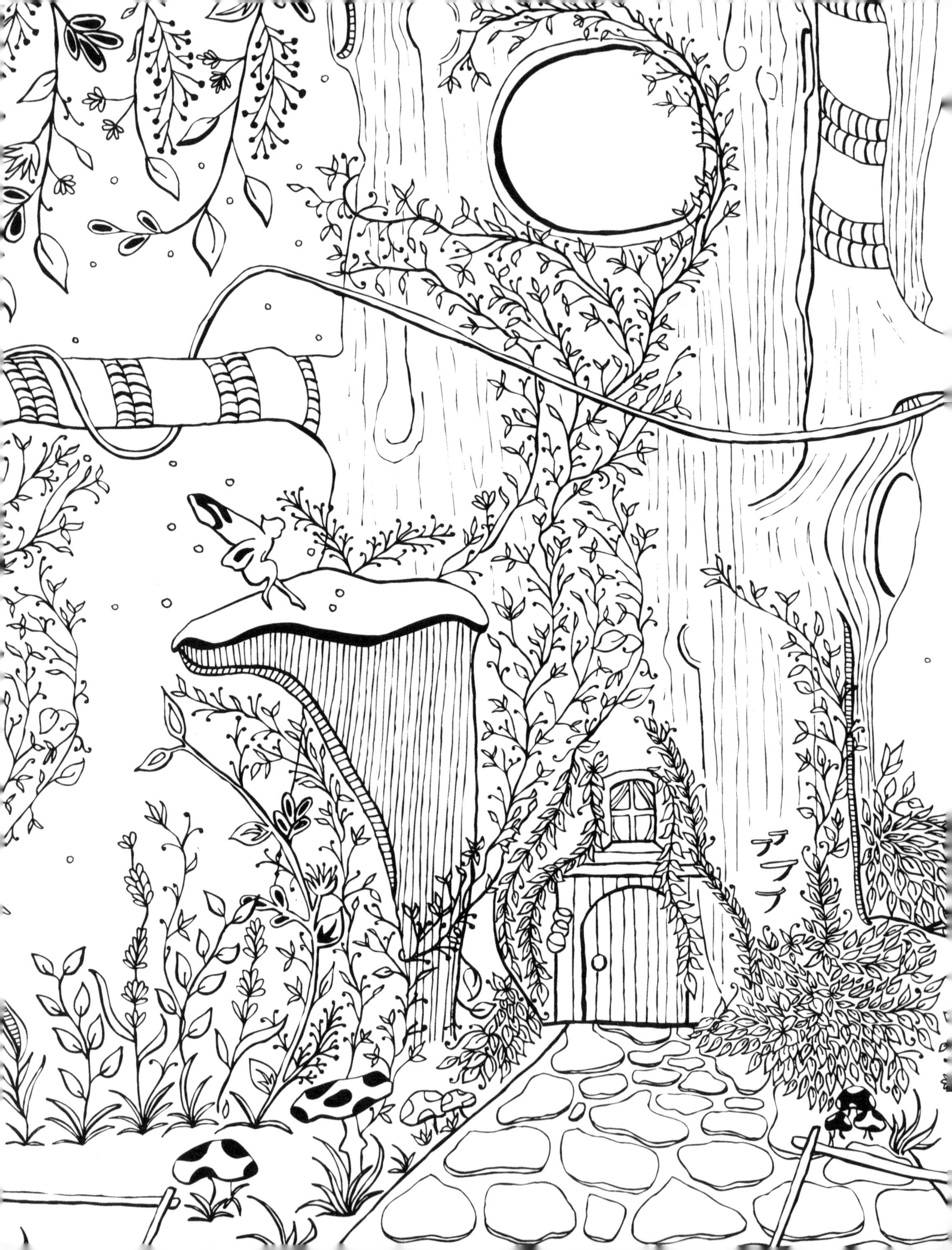

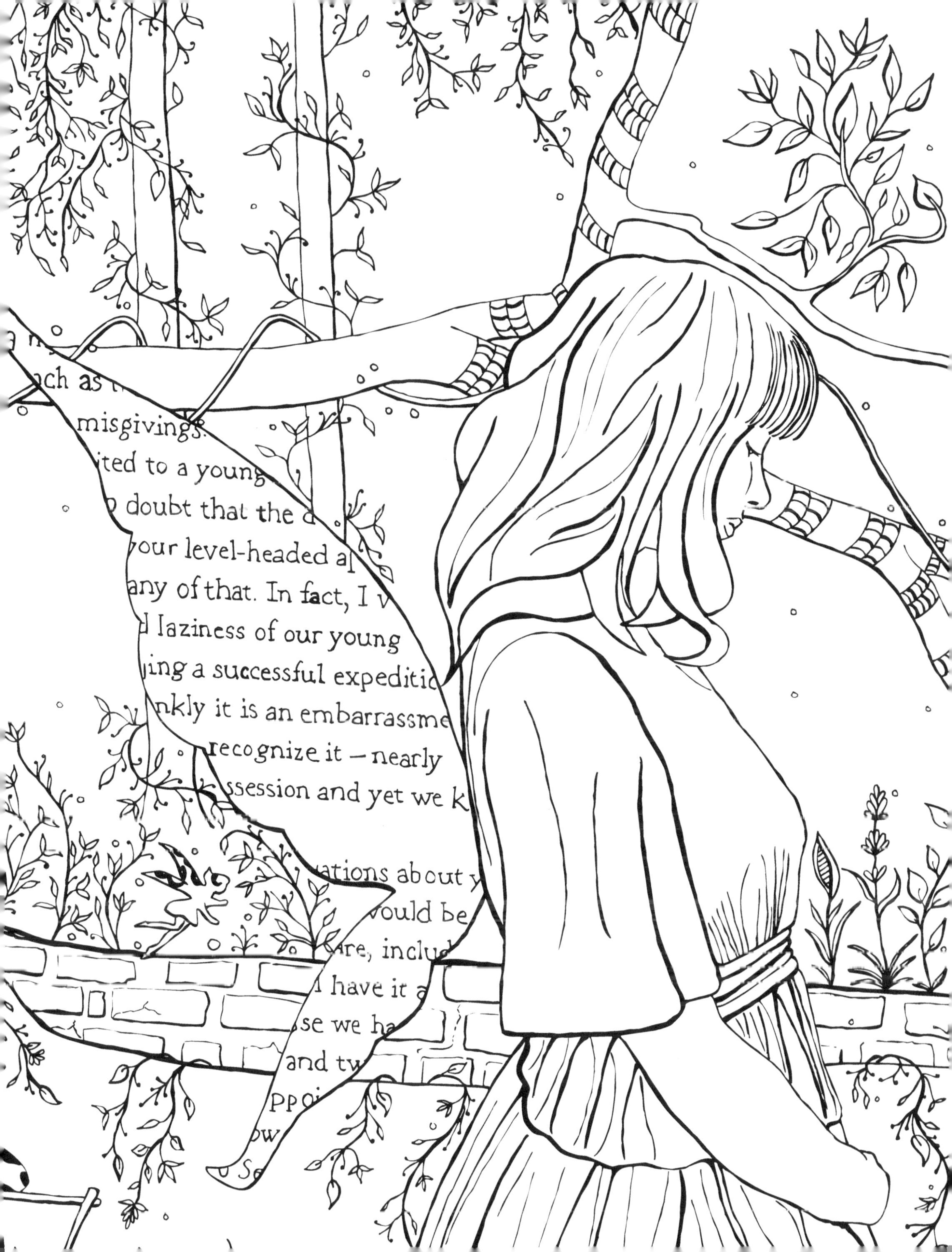
misgivings.
ited to a young
doubt that the
our level-headed a
any of that. In fact, I
laziness of our young
ing a successful expediti
nkly it is an embarrassme
recognize it — nearly
ssession and yet we k
ations about
ould be
re, includ
have it
se we ha
and tw
ppoi
w

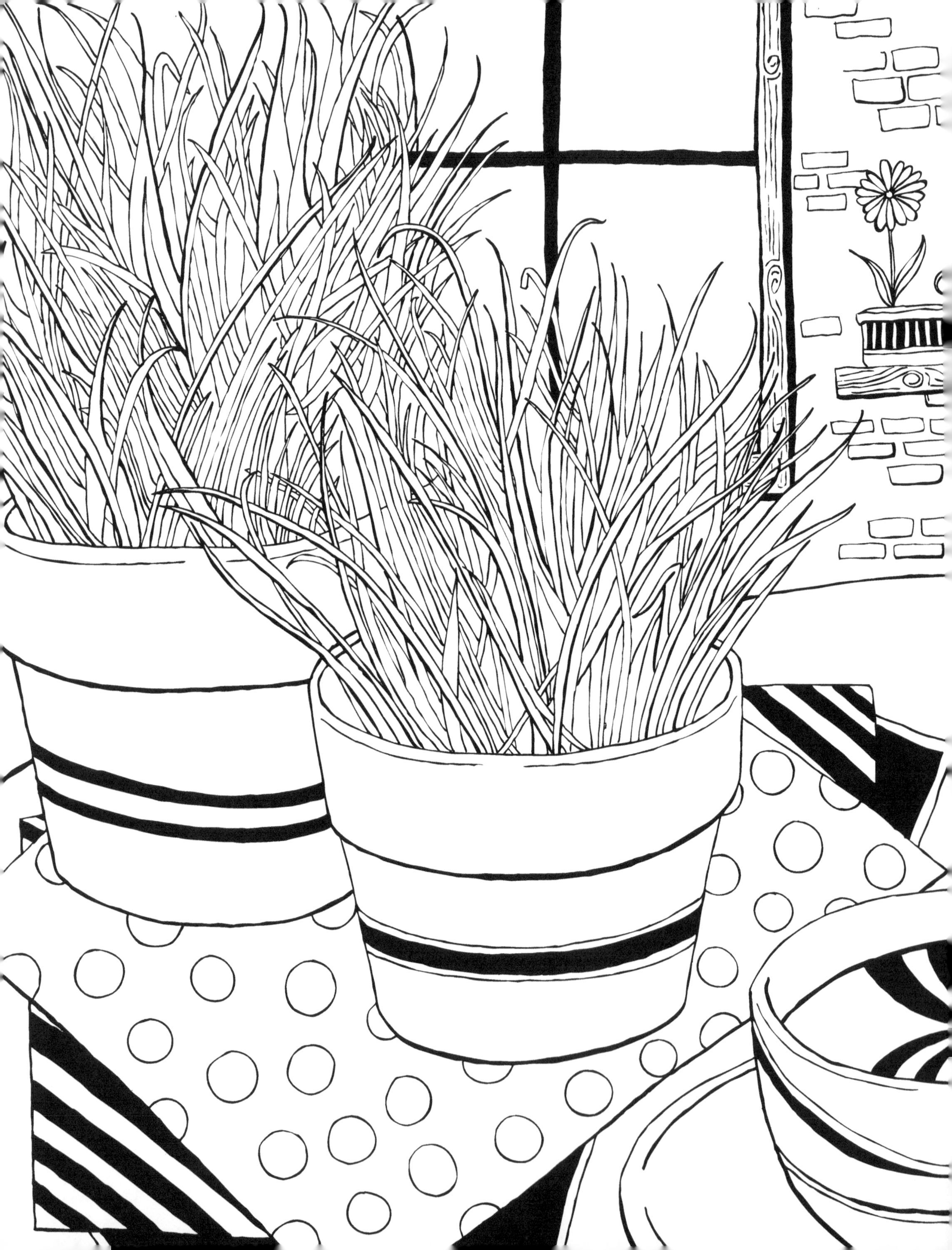

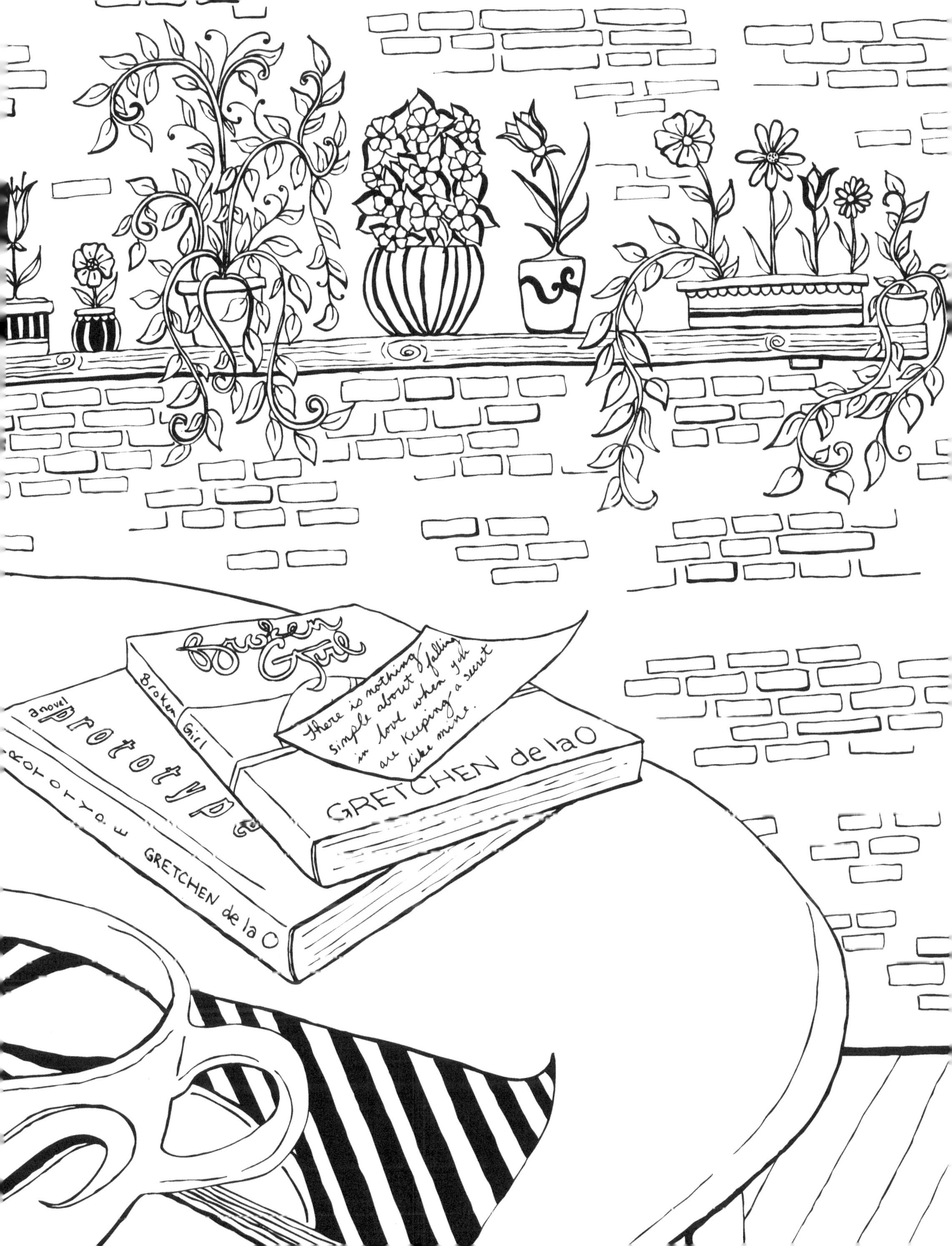

Broken Girl
Broken Girl
a novel
prototype
prototype
GRETCHEN de la O
GRETCHEN de la O
There is nothing falling simple about in love when you are keeping a secret like mine.

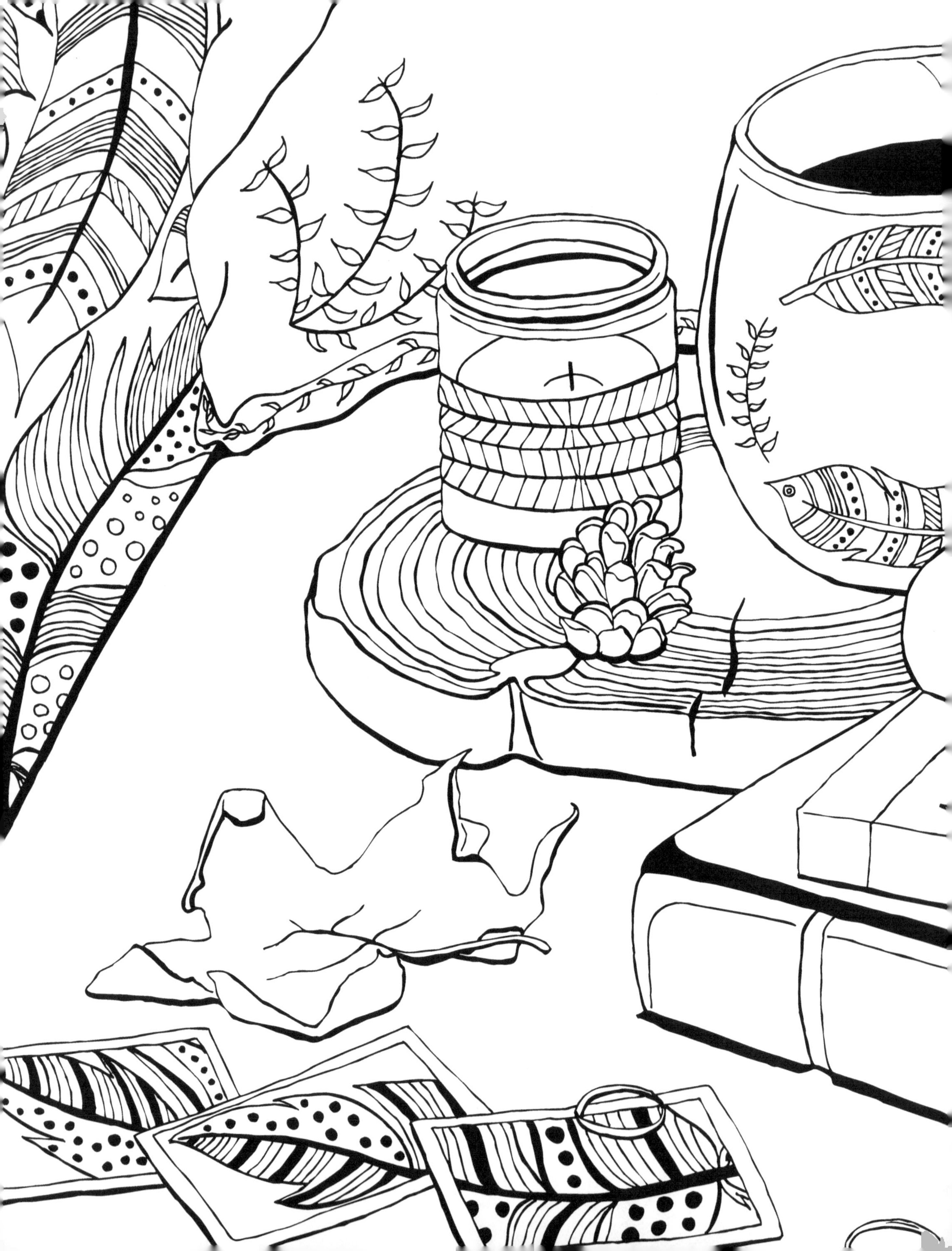

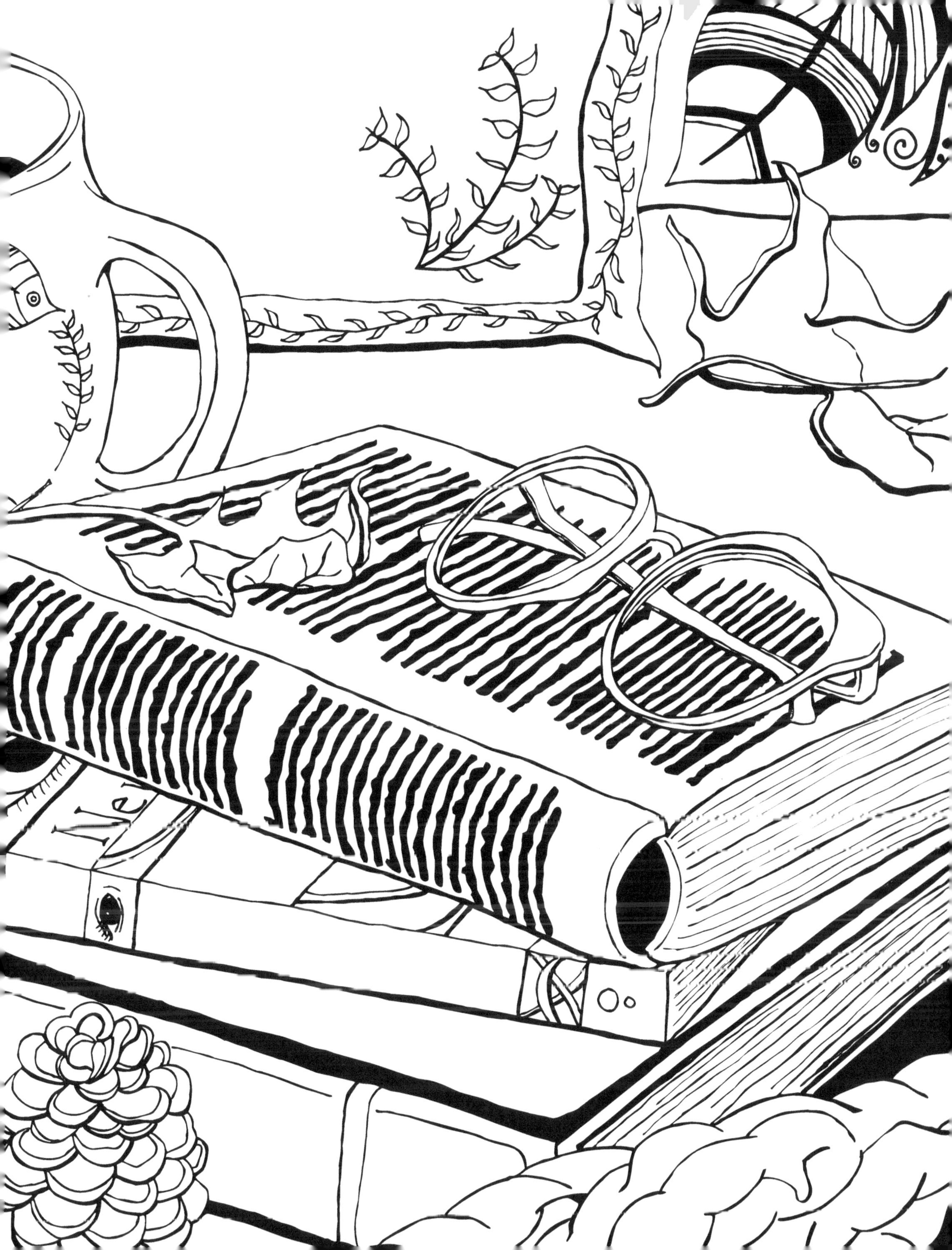

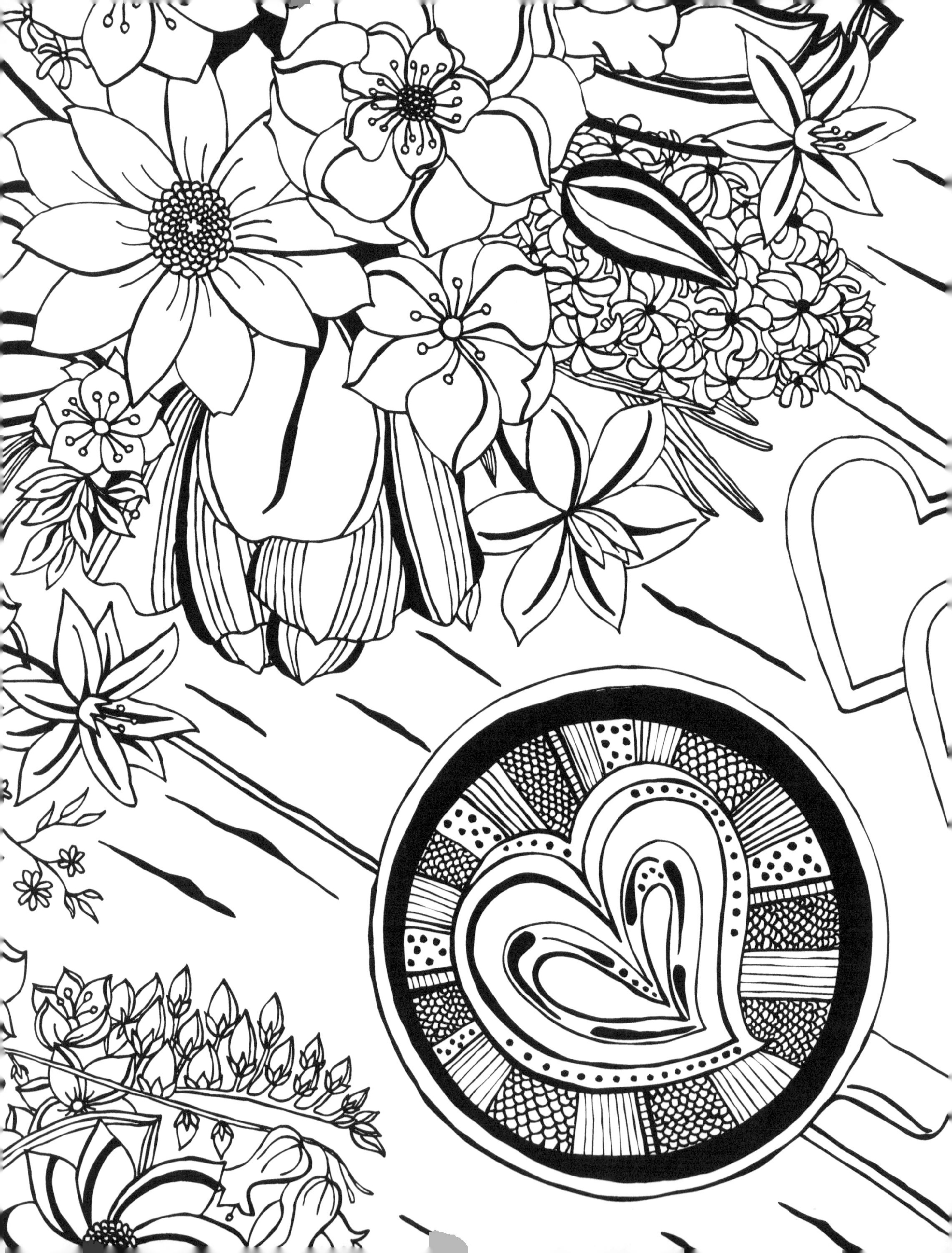

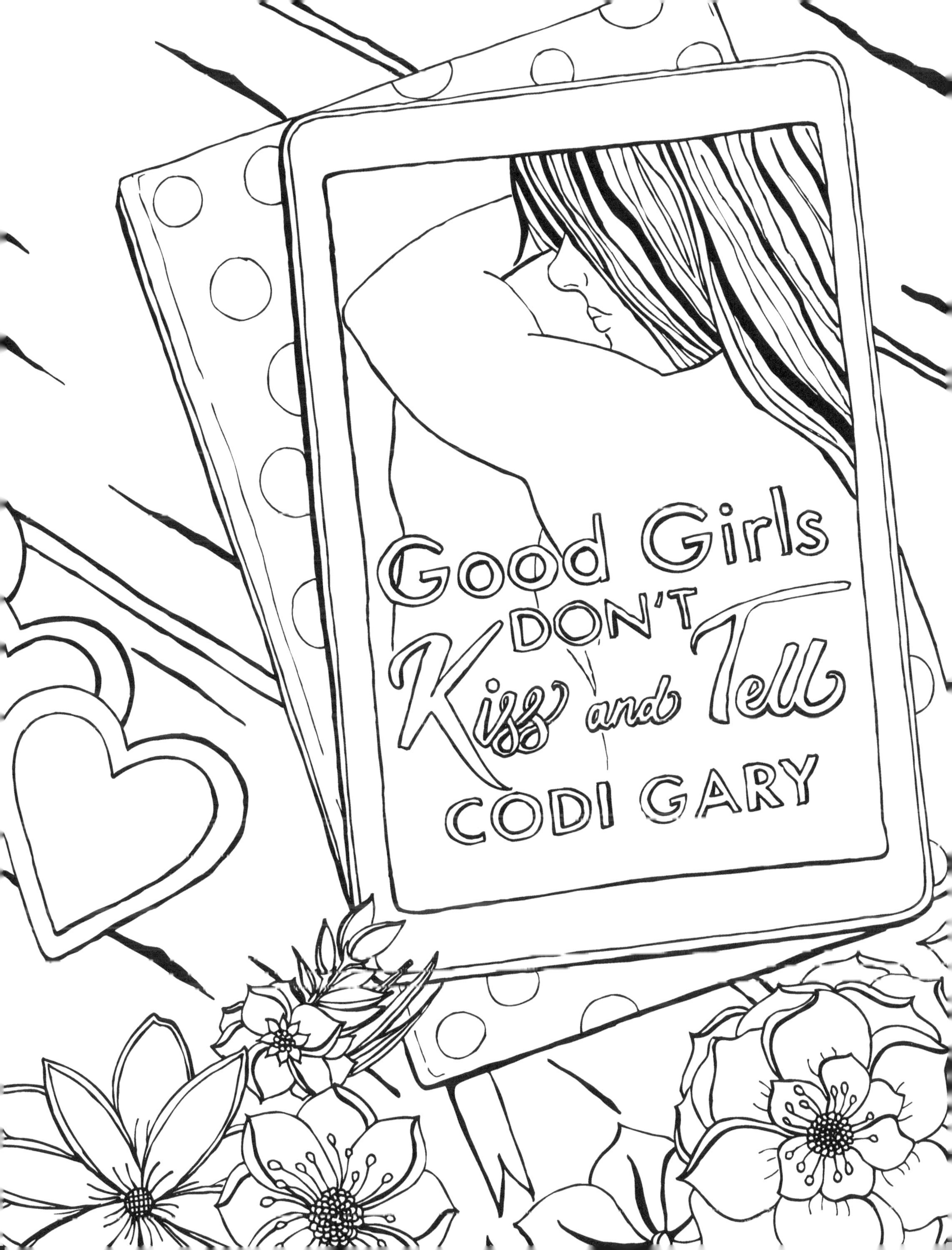

Good Girls
DON'T
Kiss and Tell
CODI GARY

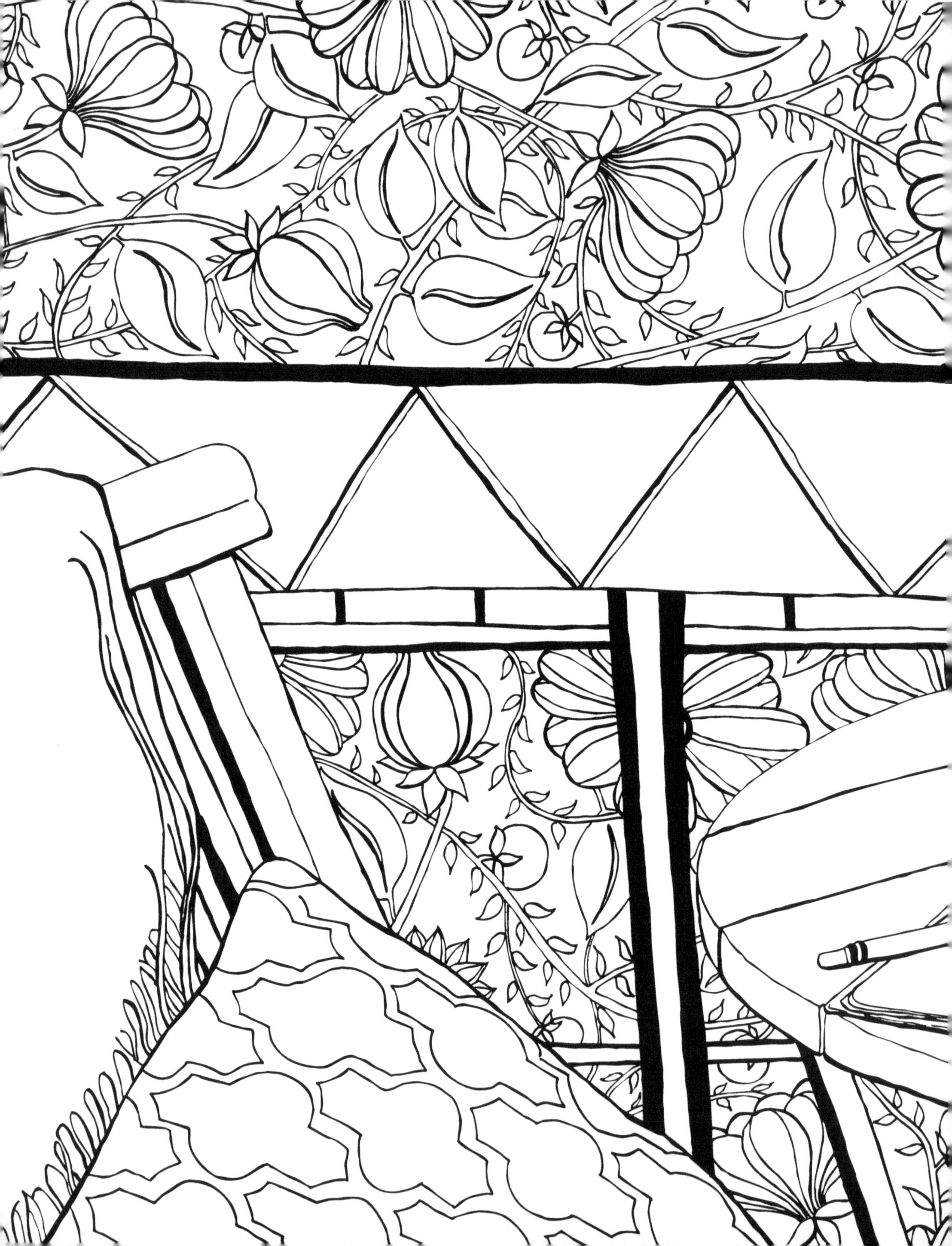

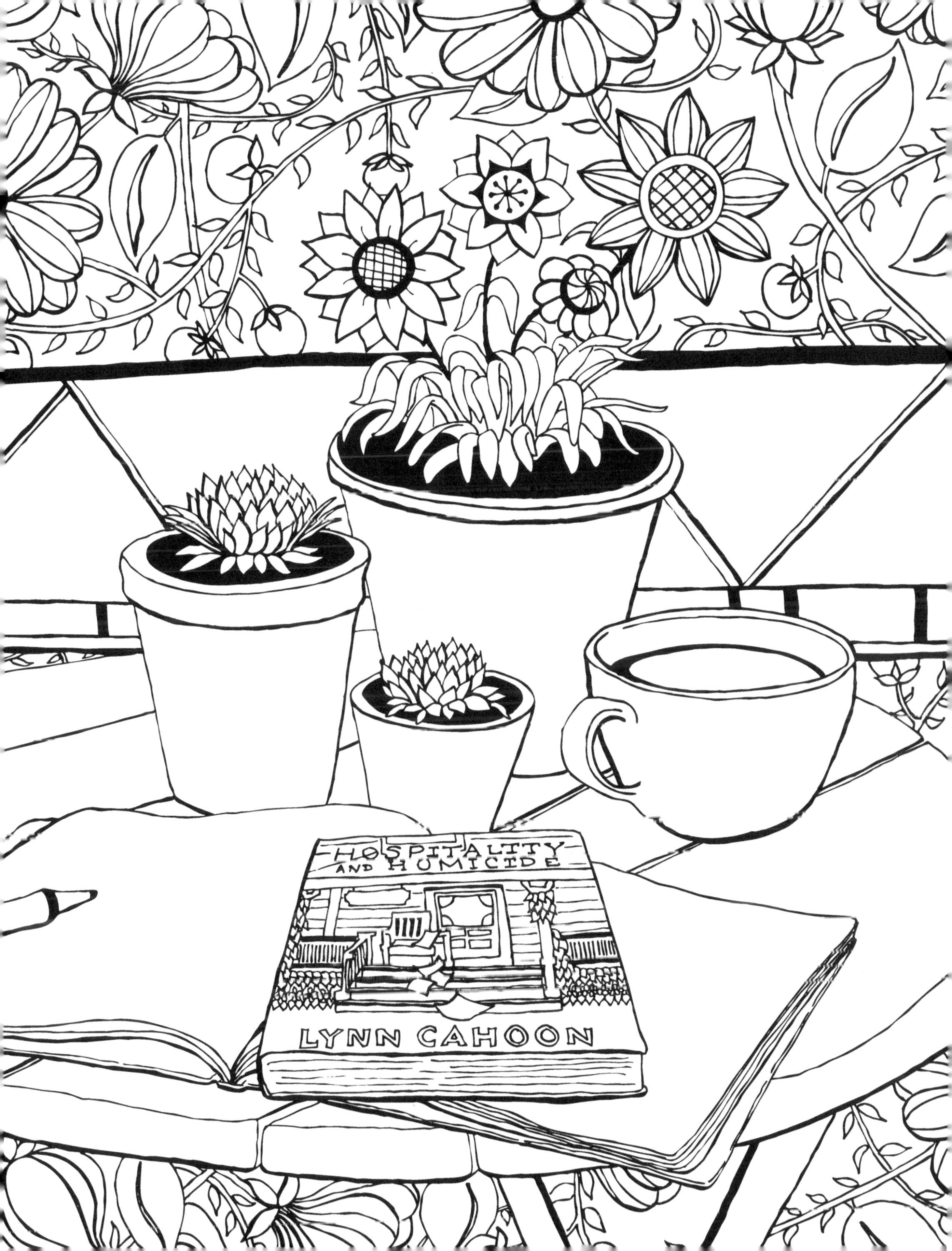

HOSPITALITY
AND HOMICIDE
LYNN CAHOON

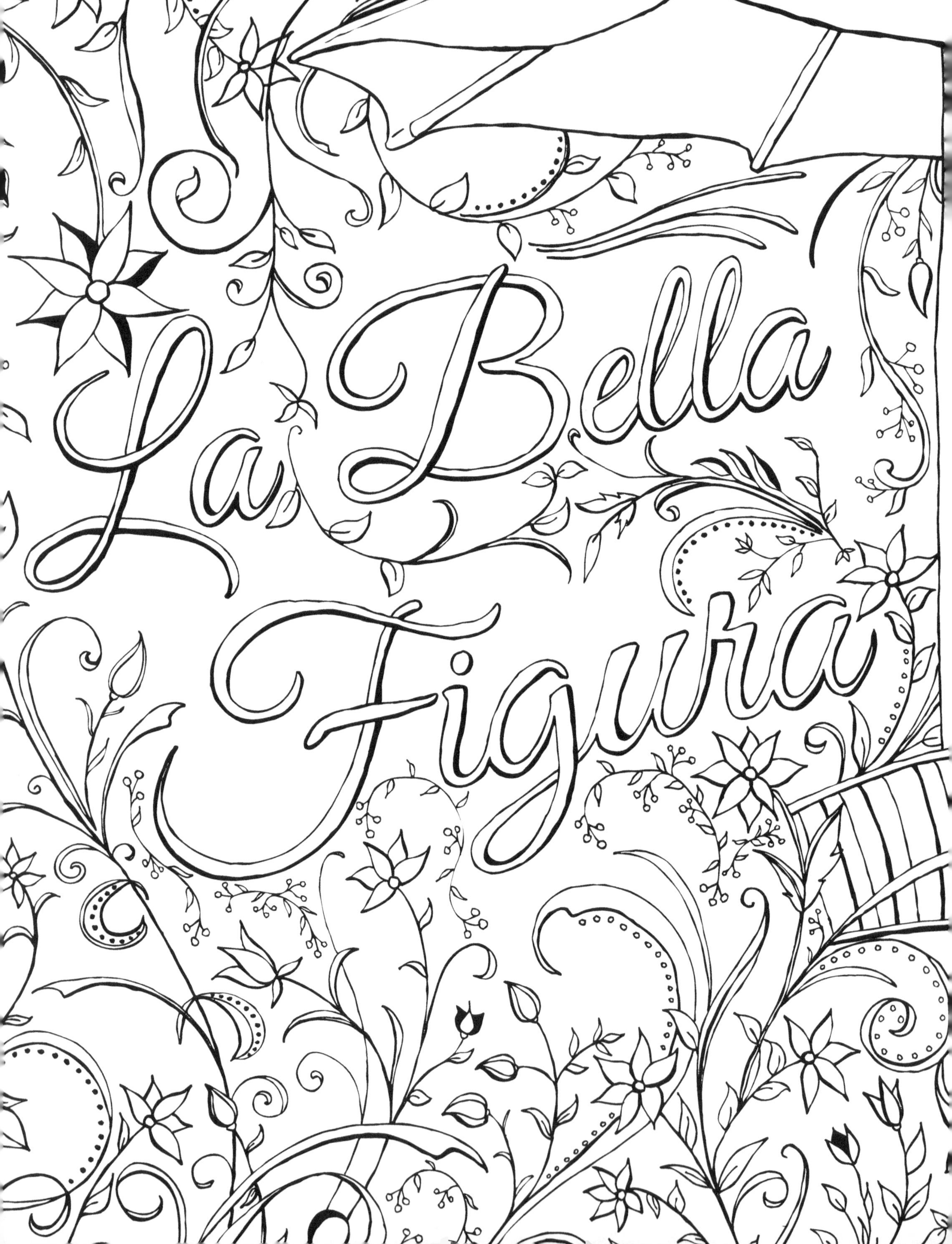

La Bella
Figura

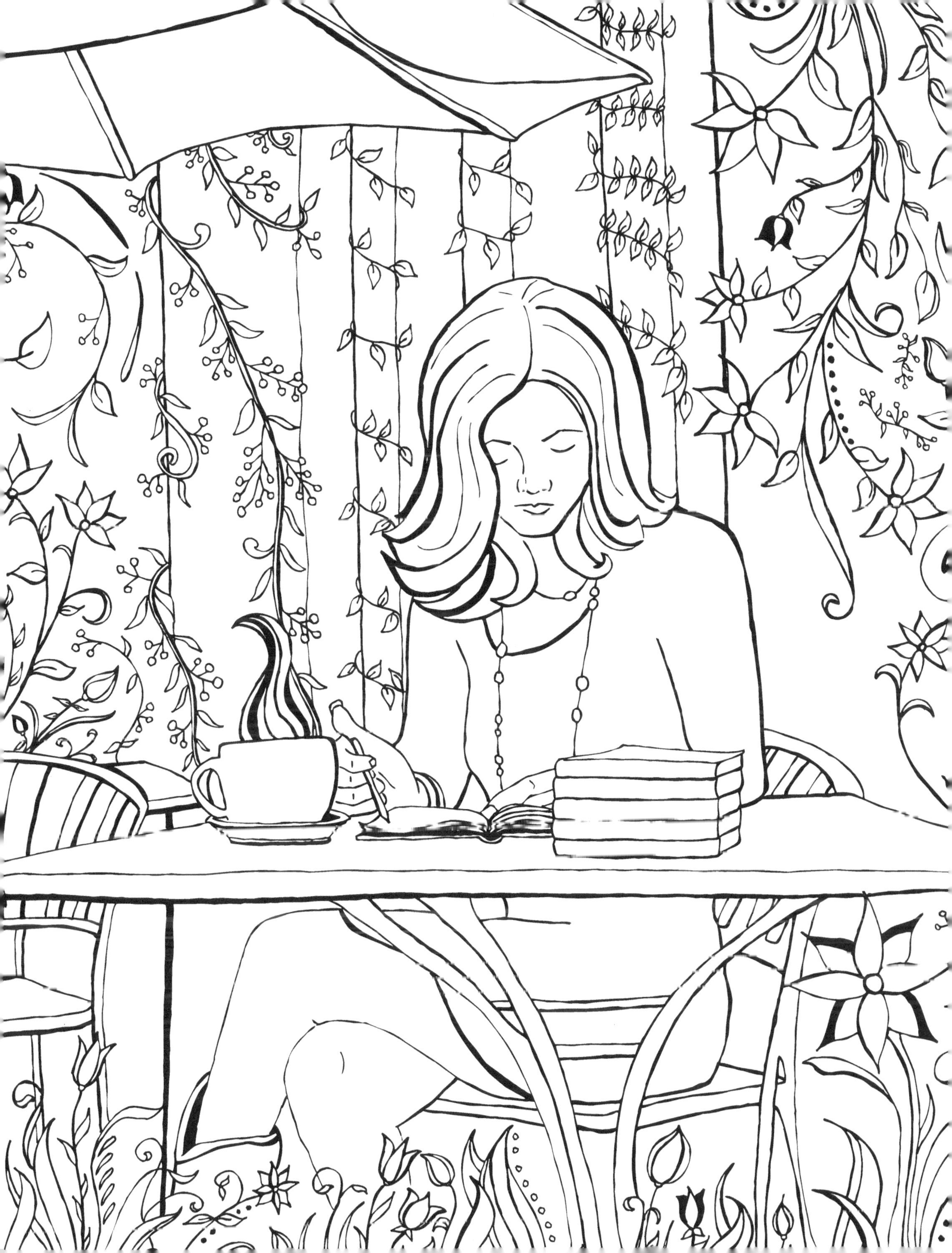

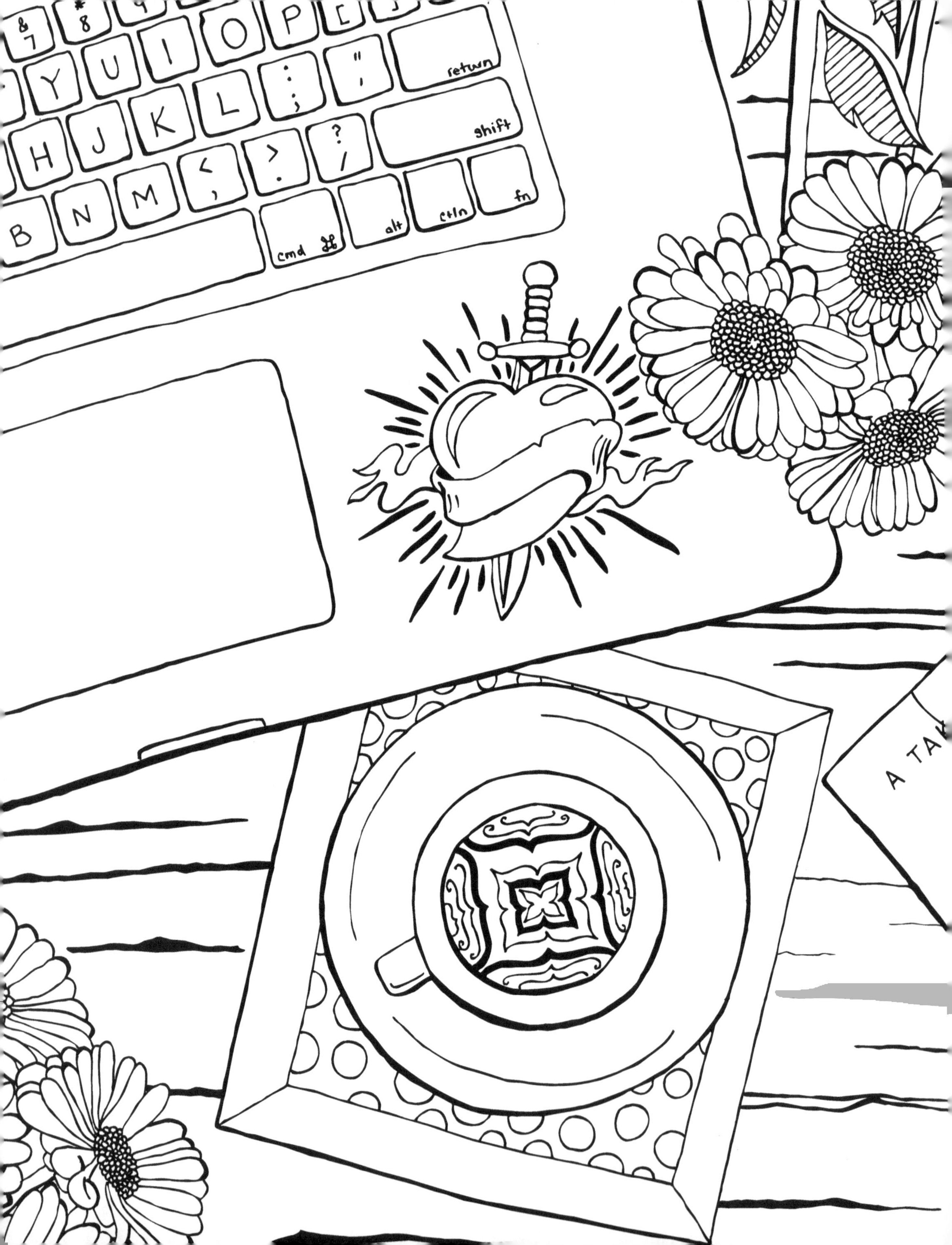

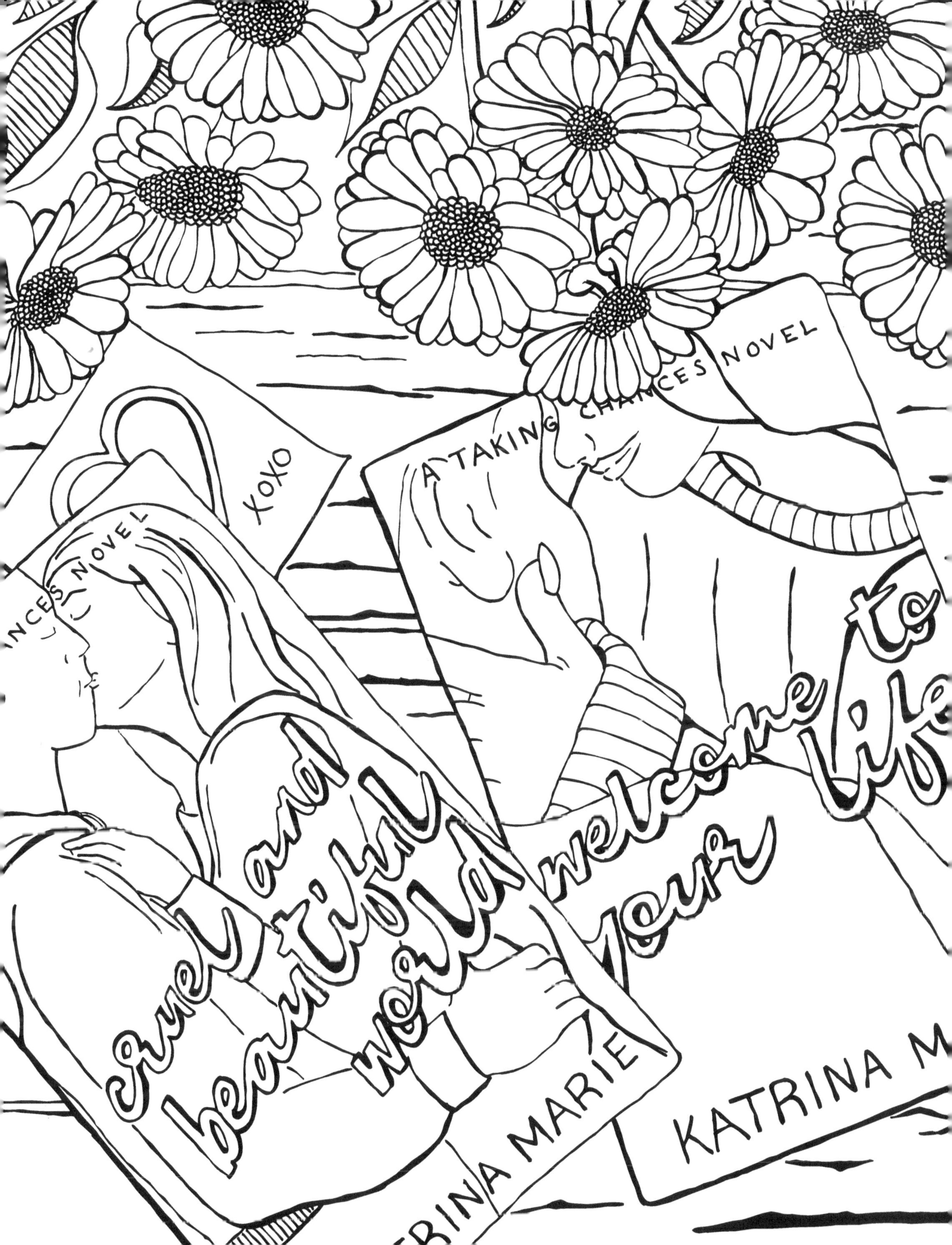
A TAKING CHANCES NOVEL
...NCES NOVEL
...INCES NOVEL
XOXO
sweet and
beautiful
world welcome to
your life
KATRINA MARIE
...TRINA MARIE
KATRINA M

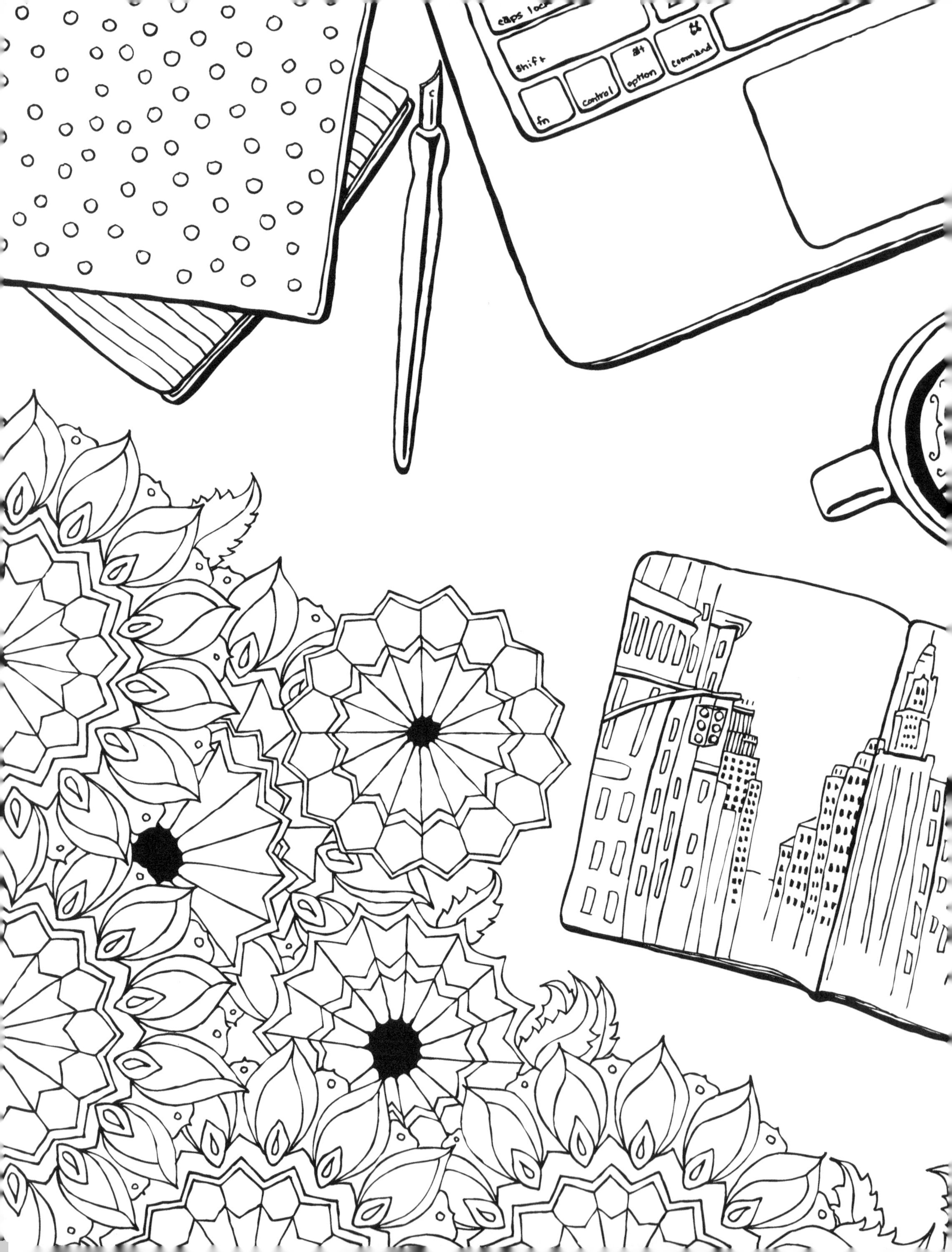

caps lock
shift
fn
control
option
command

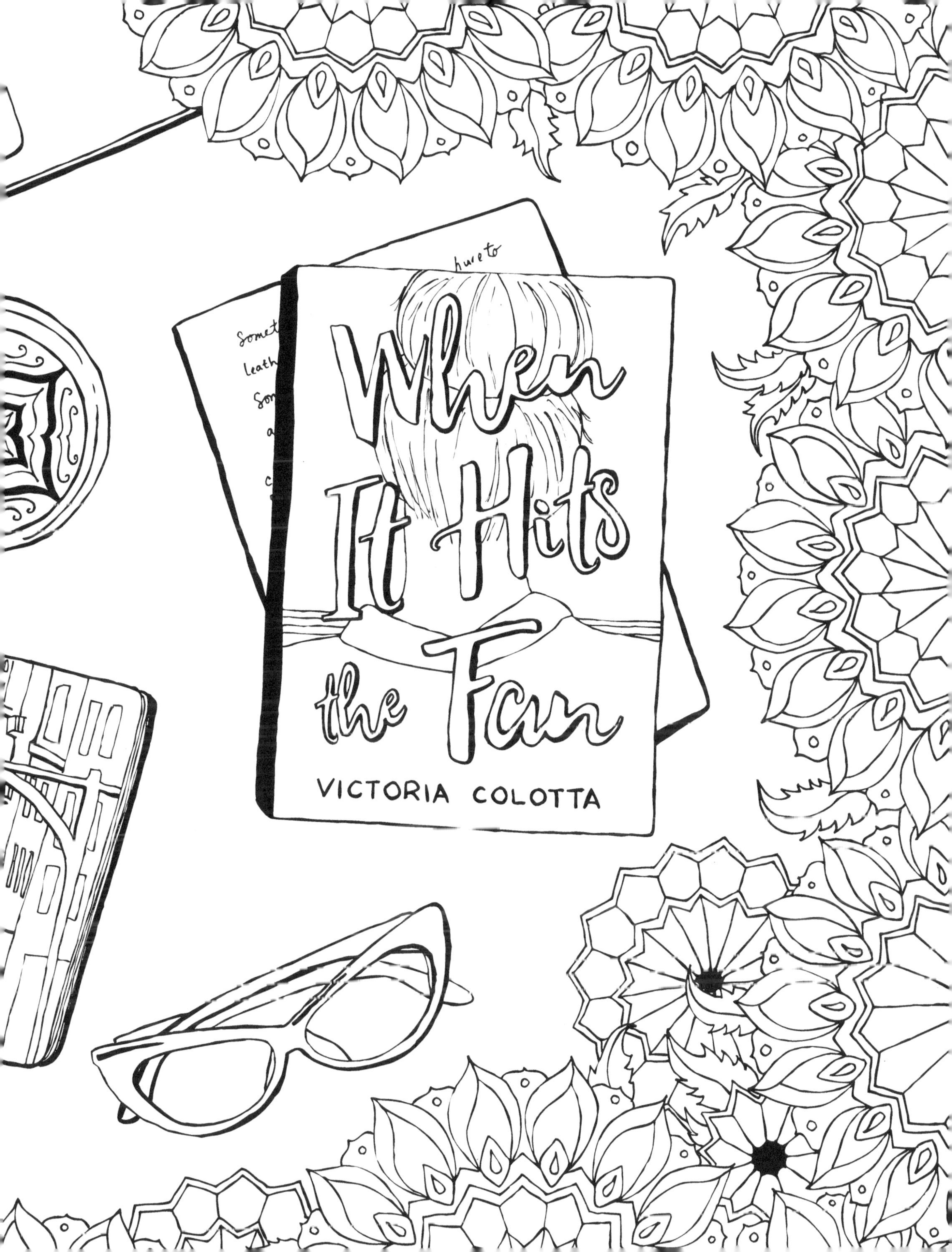

When It Hits the Fan
VICTORIA COLOTTA

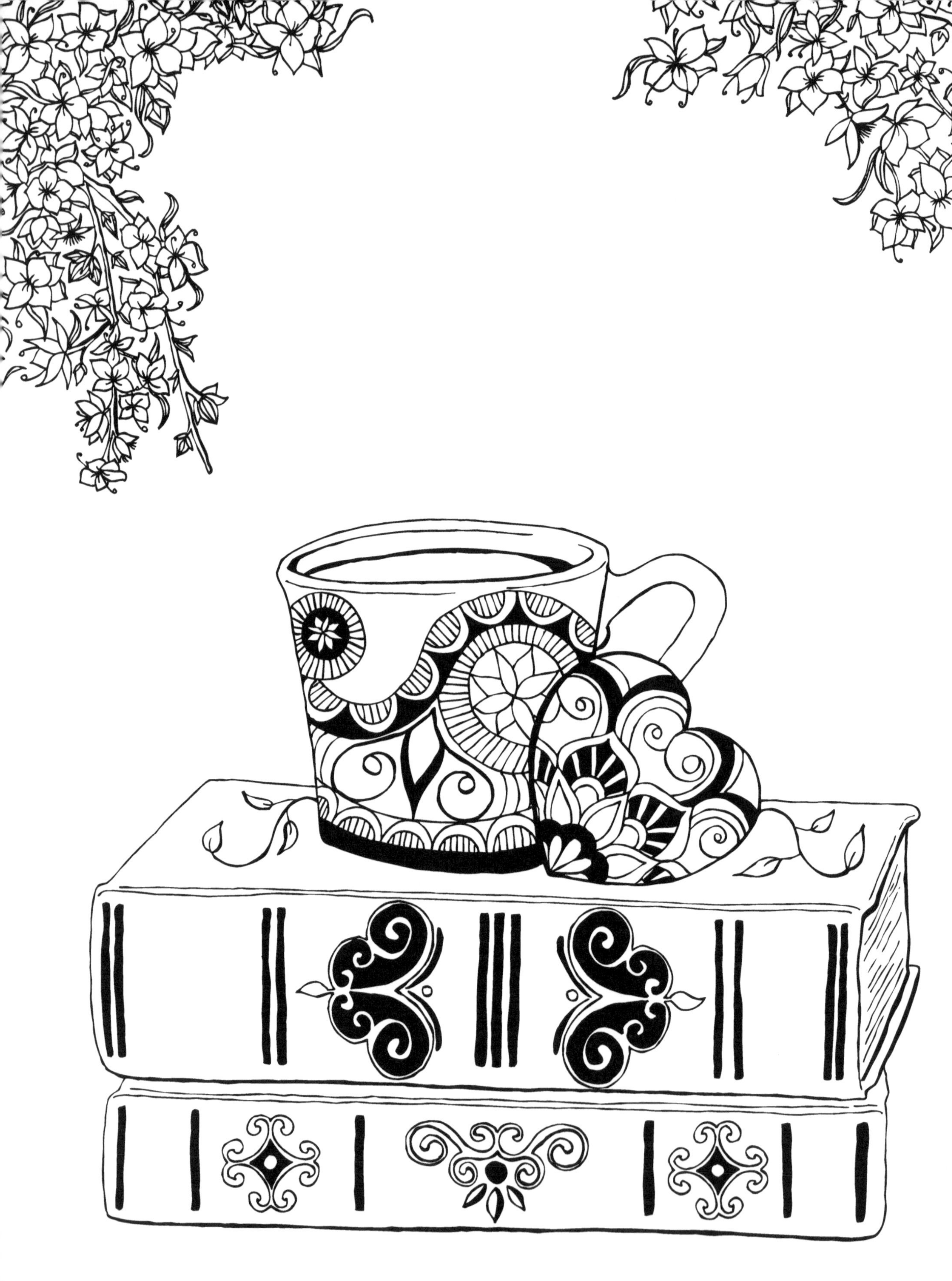

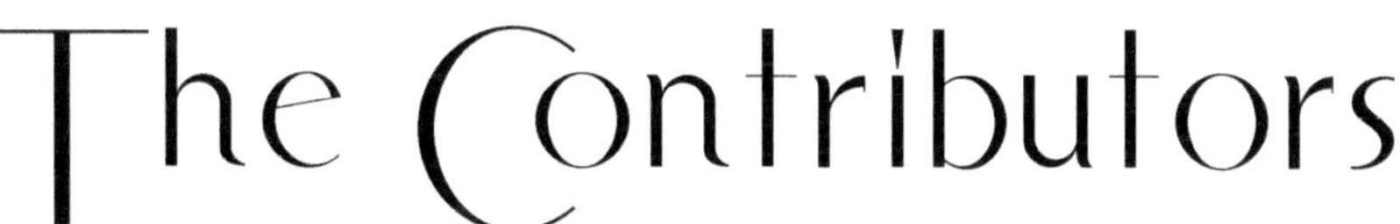

# The Contributors

A special thank you to all the bookstagrammers and authors who were excited to participate in the book. Here is a little more about these amazingly talented people and where you can follow them!

## Bookstagrammers

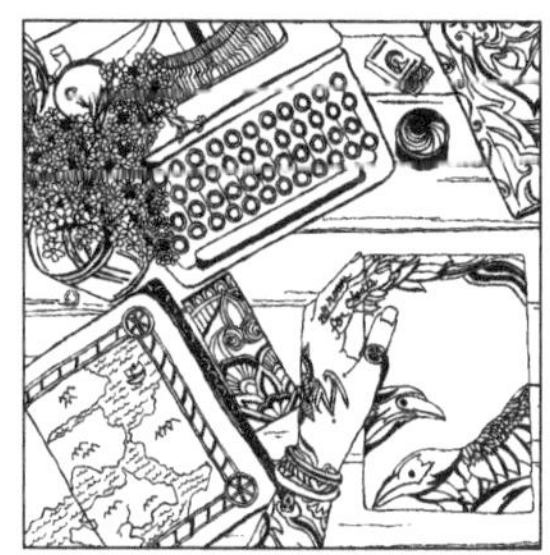

### URSULA URIARTE

@ursula_uriarte

Mom, bookworm, traveler, and metalhead. #urstravels

instagram.com/ursula_uriarte

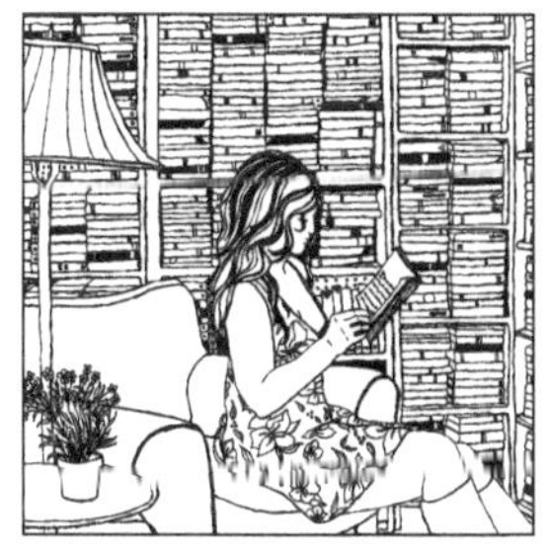

### CARMEN DESIREE SEDA

@carmdesiree

books | travel | decor | lifestyle

Carmen is a literary-based influencer who curates and photographs books and other related content.

instagram.com/carmdesiree • sociallycarmen.com

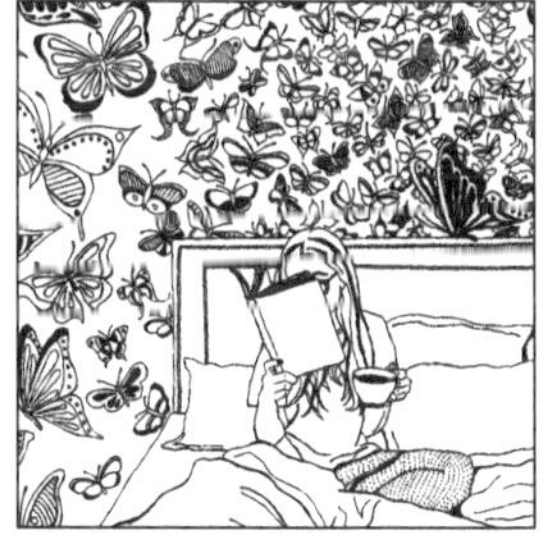

### NATASHA, BOOK BARISTAS

@BookBaristas

Just a book person recommending you hot drinks and hotter reads. Natasha Miñoso is a full-time book person marketing books at work and on @BookBaristas. You can probably find her at a bagel store in Brooklyn on the weekends. She is also the co-founder of She is Booked (@sheisbooked).

instagram.com/bookbaristas • bookbaristas.org

instagram.com/sheisbooked • sheisbooked.com

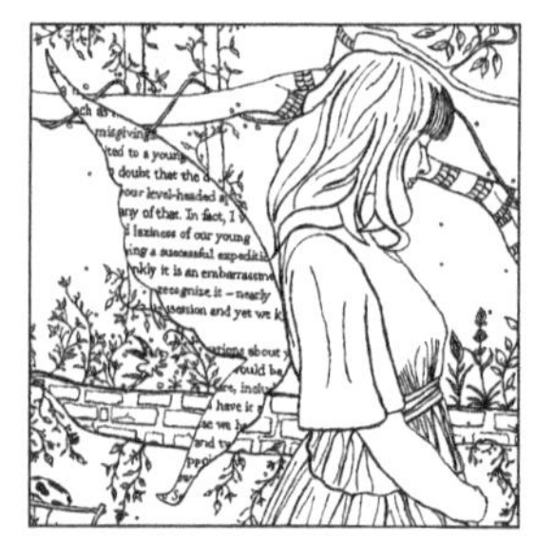

## BRONTE (BEE)

@frombeewithlove

Storyteller, Creative & Miniature Artist

Romantic & Whimsical meets Strange & Unusual.

Bronte's whimsical, nostalgic style of photography is mixed with a love of books, adventures, fashion, and entertainment to form a unique, eclectic style. Her accompanying writing is character-driven and she touches on subjects often not discussed in the mainstream media, all mixed with a dose of creativity, sarcasm, and wittiness.

instagram.com/frombeewithlove • frombeewithlove.com

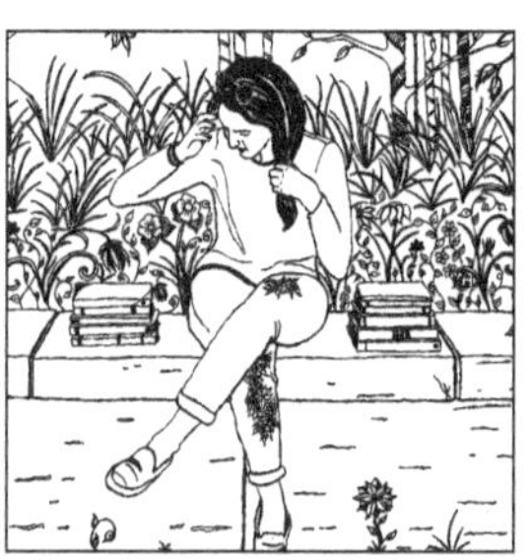

## MORGAN PAGER

@nycbookgirl

lover of literary fiction, strong coffee, #jumpsuitthursday, & theater.

Morgan Hoit is the content creator and book worm behind nycbookgirl—a blog dedicated to book recommendations, guides to NYC, and more. Morgan is also the Associate Marketing Manager at Avid Reader Press, where she is the voice of the imprint on social media and also manages title marketing campaigns, working closely with authors on their digital presence and social media strategy.

instagram.com/nycbookgirl • nycbookgirl.com

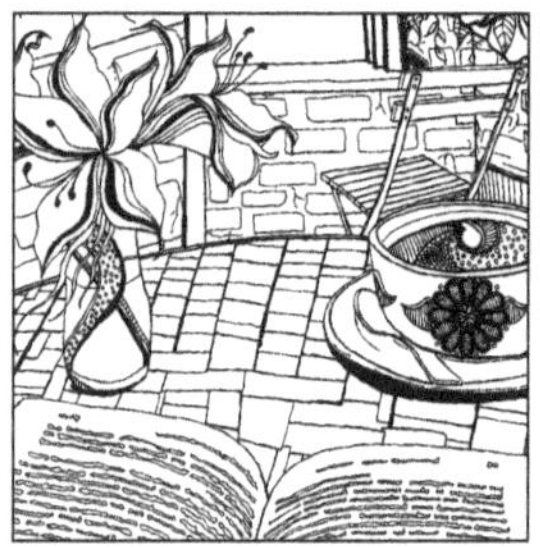

## ABBY, CRIME BY THE BOOK

@crimebythebook

A girl investigates crime fiction from around the world, by the book.

Abby has been a crime fiction fan ever since her first discovered her mom's childhood collection of Nancy Drew books hiding in a dusty box in their attic. After going on one adventure with the strawberry-blonde sleuth, she was hooked. She has been exploring the best (and worst) in crime fiction ever since.

instagram.com/crimebythebook • crimebythebook.com

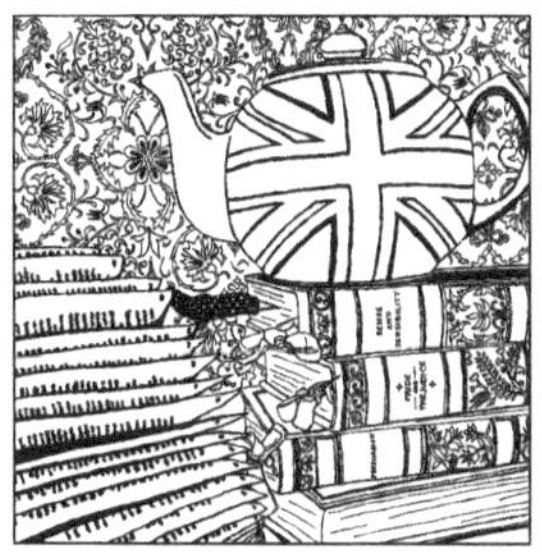

## TRIIN VIHUR

@wordchild

Avid reader, passionate photographer. Thrives on a steady diet of books, films, and music.

instagram.com/wordchild • word-child.com

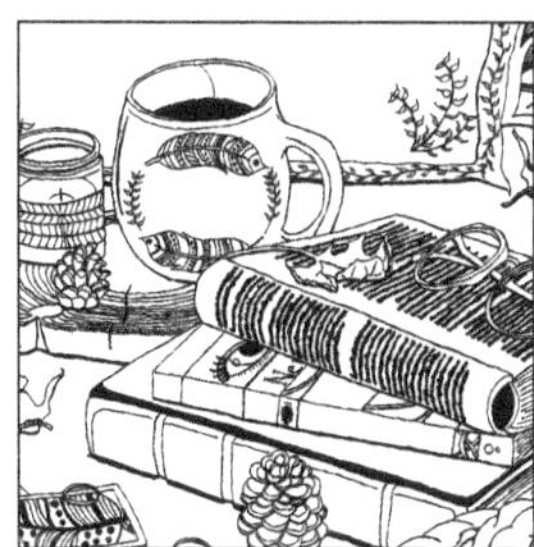

## POLLY FLORENCE

@polly.florence

Polly is a photographer and online content creator based in the UK with a love for all things books, travel, and cozy interiors.

instagram.com/polly.florence • pollyflorence.com

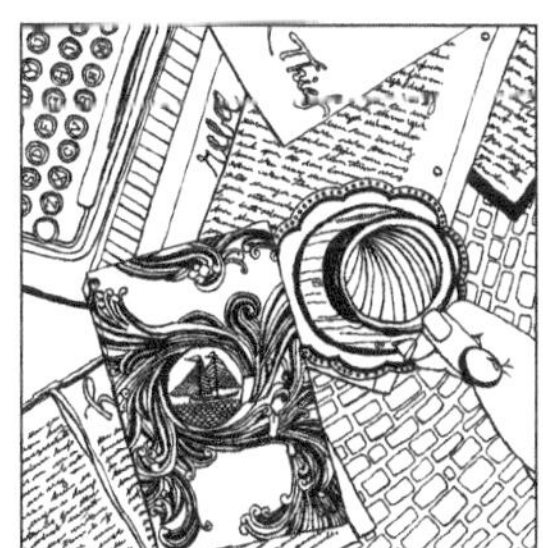

## CICELY V. FORD

@cicelyvford

avid reader & reviewer

unapologetic lover of autumn

instagram.com/cicelyvford

# Authors

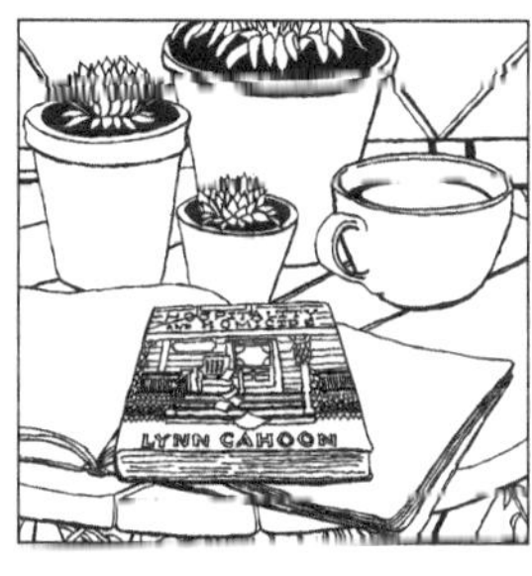

## LYNN CAHOON

*New York Times* and *USA Today* bestselling author Lynn Cahoon started her career writing sweet contemporary romances with heroes ranging from cowboys to warlocks. Since 2014, Lynn has created three bestselling cozy mystery series—The Tourist Trap Mysteries, The Cat Latimer Mysteries Series, and The Farm-to-Fork Mysteries Series. An over ten-year breast cancer survivor, she lives in a small town like the ones she loves to write about with her husband and three fur babies.

lynncahoon.com • instagram.com/lynncahoon

Bruce Emmett, Cover Illustrator for HOSPITALITY AND HOMICIDE

bruceemmett.blogspot.com

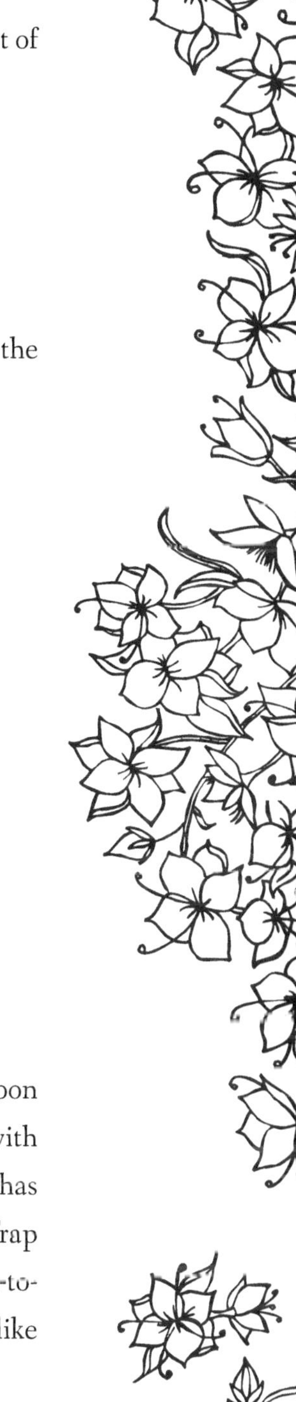

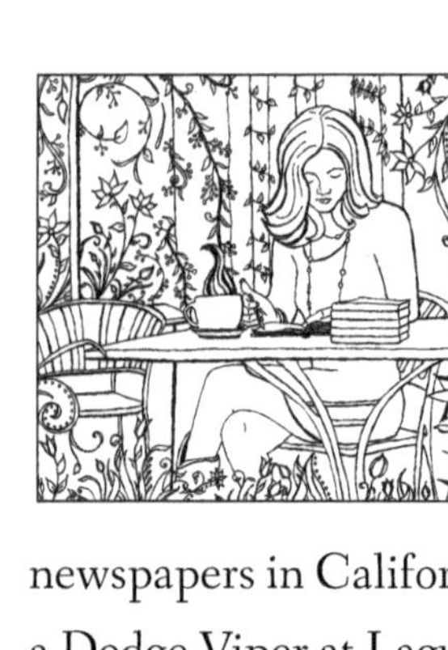

## KRISTI BELCAMINO

*USA Today* Bestselling author and Agatha, Anthony, Barry, and Macavity Award Finalist Kristi Belcamino writes dark mysteries about fierce women seeking justice. She is a crime fiction writer, cops beat reporter, and Italian mama who also bakes a tasty biscotti. In her former life, as an award-winning crime reporter at newspapers in California, she flew over Big Sur in an FA-18 jet with the Blue Angels, raced a Dodge Viper at Laguna Seca, and attended barbecues at the morgue.

kristibelcaminowriter.com • instagram.com/kristibelcaminobooks

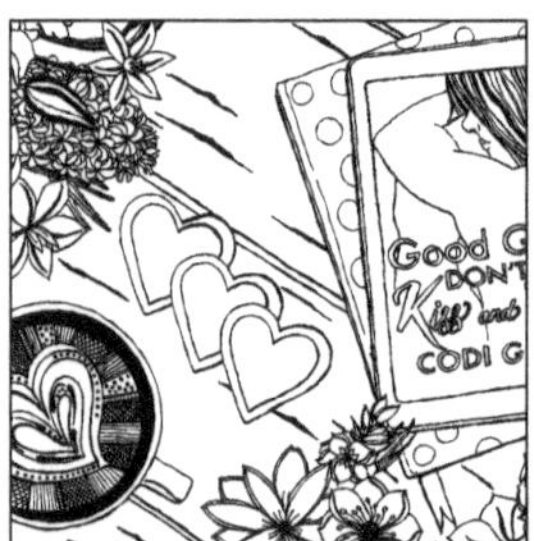

## CODI GARY

Codi Gary loves writing books almost as much as she loves outings with her family and snuggling with her adorable fur babies. An RWA Honor Roll author of more than twenty romance novels and novellas, her goals are to make her readers laugh one minute and cry the next in the best way possible. When she isn't glued to her computer, she can be found reading fantastic books, catching up on all the shows she loves, and taking pictures of her beautiful kids. To keep up with her releases, cover reveals, and crazy antics, just go to her website at www.codigarysbooks.com and sign up for her newsletter.

codigarysbooks.com • instagram.com/authorcodihallgary

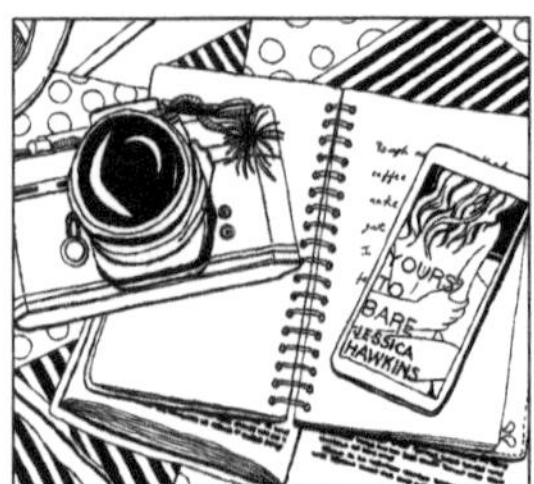

## JESSICA HAWKINS

Jessica Hawkins is a *USA Today* bestselling author known for her "emotionally gripping" and "off-the-charts hot" romance. Dubbed "queen of angst" by both peers and readers for her smart and provocative work, she's garnered a cult-like following of fans who love to be torn apart...and put back together. She writes romance both at home in New York City and around the world.

jessicahawkins.net • instagram.com/jessica_hawkins

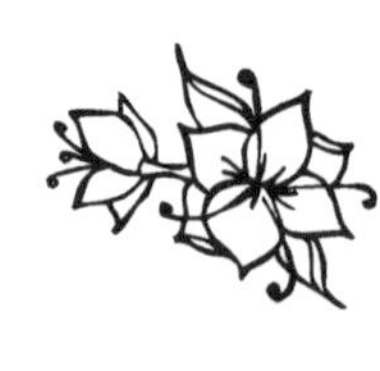

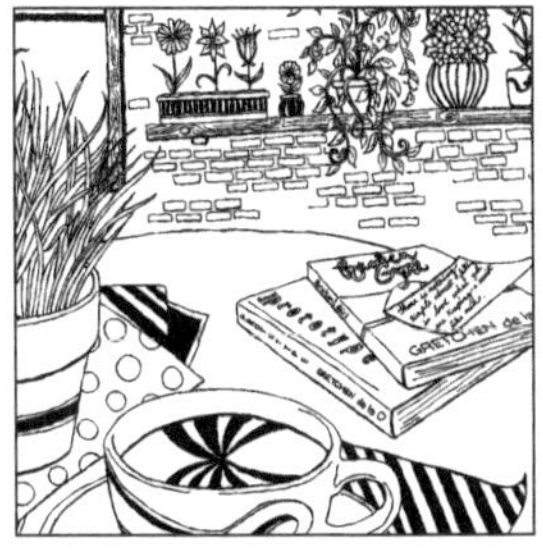

## GRETCHEN DE LA O

Gretchen de la O is an eclectic writer of romantically unique stories. A proclaimed positive energy infuser by people who know her, she finds joy in helping those around her discover their creative process. Gretchen is a firm believer that anything is possible if you set your mind to it, and what you expect out of life always finds a way of showing up. She's authentic in her dedication to her own creative process, finds strength in her spirituality, and is always looking for the bright spot in every situation.

gretchendelao.com • instagram.com/gretchendelao

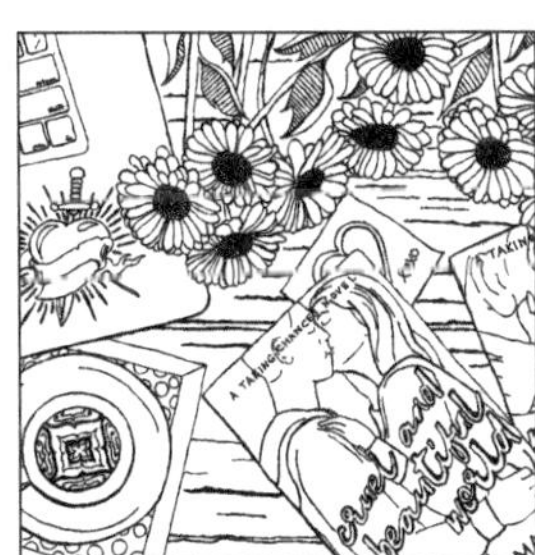

## KATRINA MARIE

Katrina Marie lives in the Dallas area with her husband, two children, and fur baby. She is a lover of all things geeky and Gryffindor for life. This is her debut novel and she hopes you enjoy reading it as much as she enjoyed writing it.

katrinamarieauthor.com • instagram.com/katrinamarieauthor

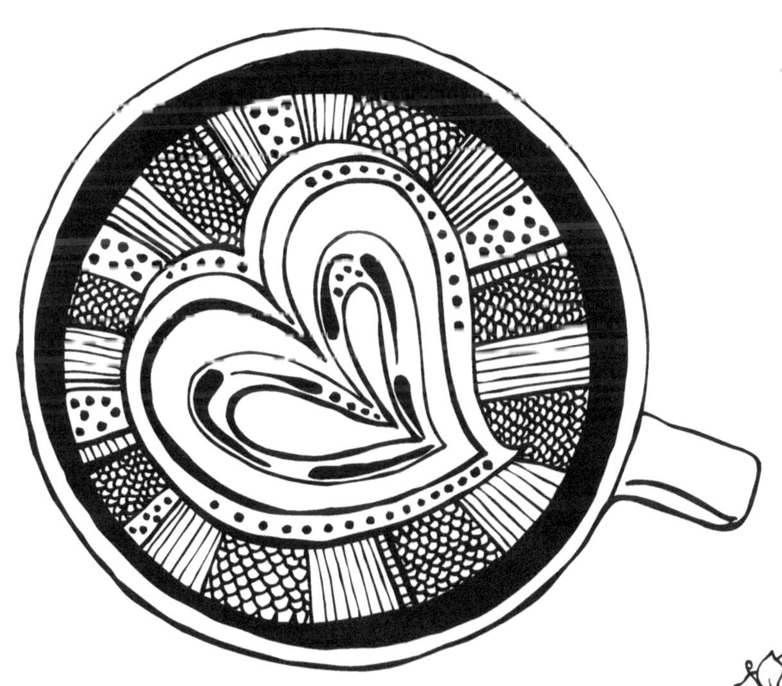

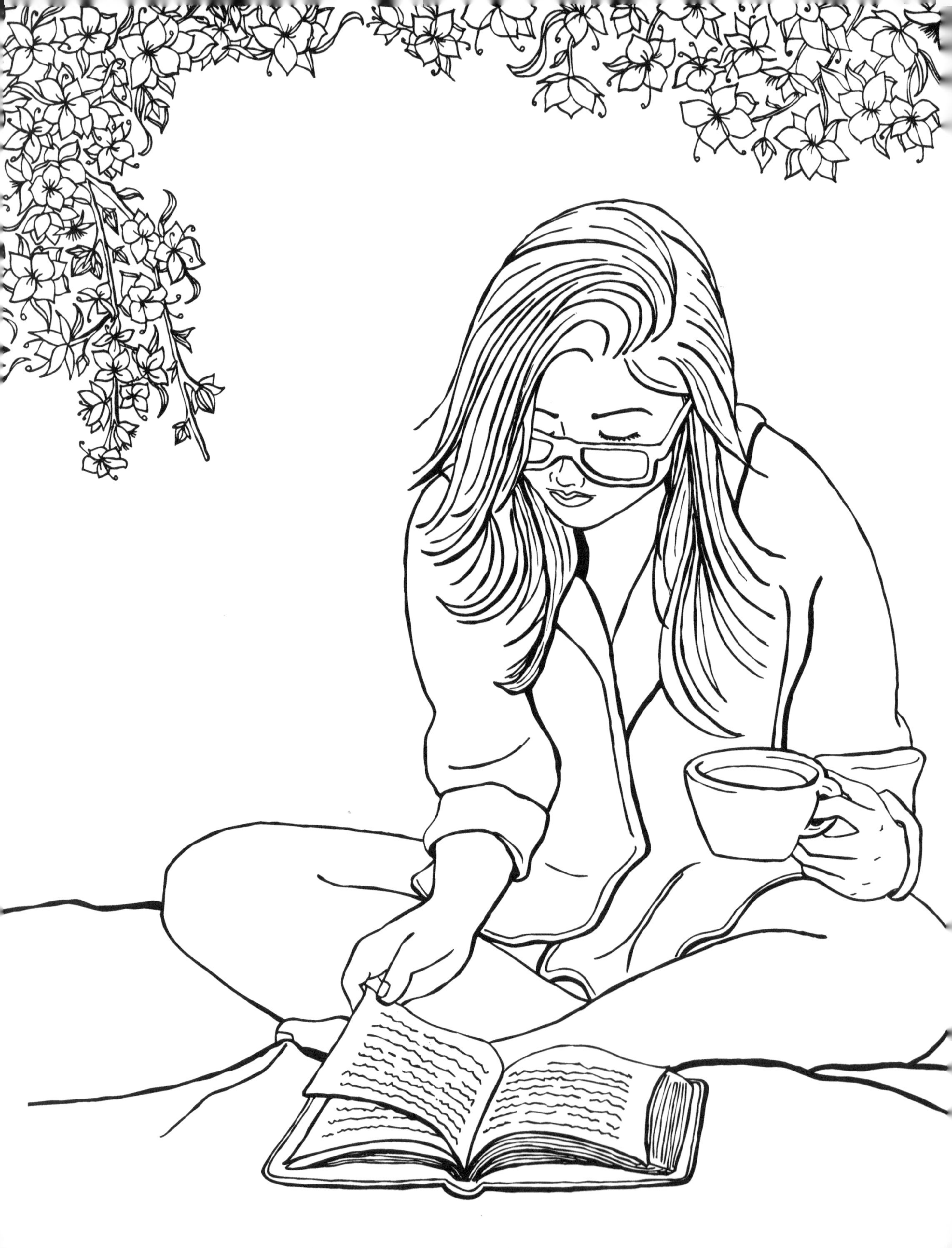

# About the Artist

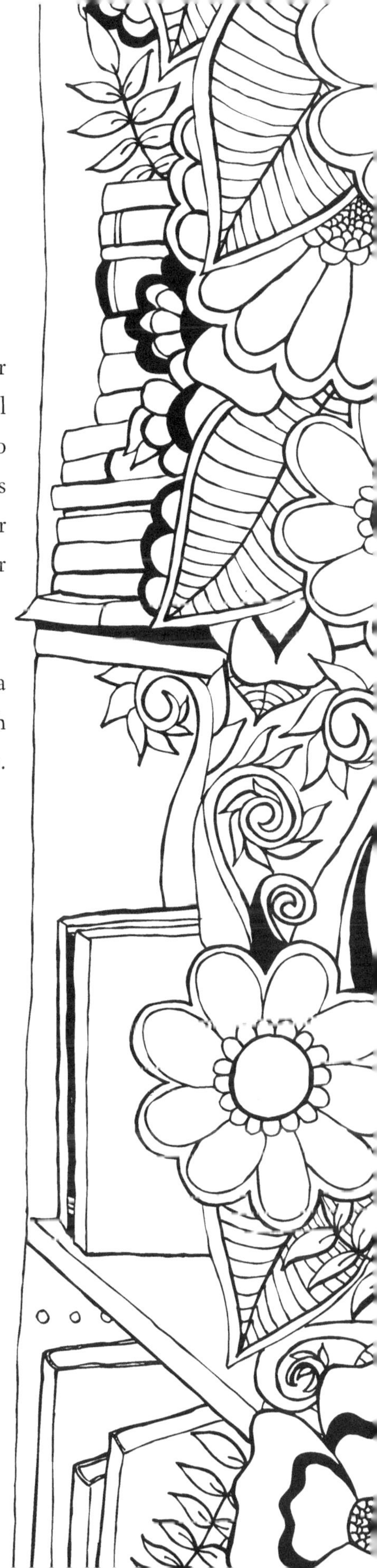

Victoria Colotta is an artist, author, and award-winning graphic designer for her work at VMC Art & Design. With a BFA from the School of Visual Arts in NYC and a voracious need to be reading, Victoria managed to merge the two loves in her life...art and books. As an artist, she is always exploring new ways to create and share her artwork. As an author, her goal is to push herself to explore all the aspecsts of her characters and their stories no matter where they may lead her.

Spending most of her day in her studio with her crazy dog Lizzy, Victoria loves to cook, bake, and read in her free time. She also enjoys talking with other readers, fellow book nerds, coffee addicts, and artists on social media.

## Follow Victoria on...

Instagram.com/artbookscoffee
Facebook.com/vcolotta
Goodreads.com/vcolotta
Behance.net/vcolotta

You can also enjoy all things Art, Books, & Coffee at artbookscoffee.substack.com and in the Art, Books, & Coffee Facebook Group (Facebook.com/groups/ArtBooksCoffee).

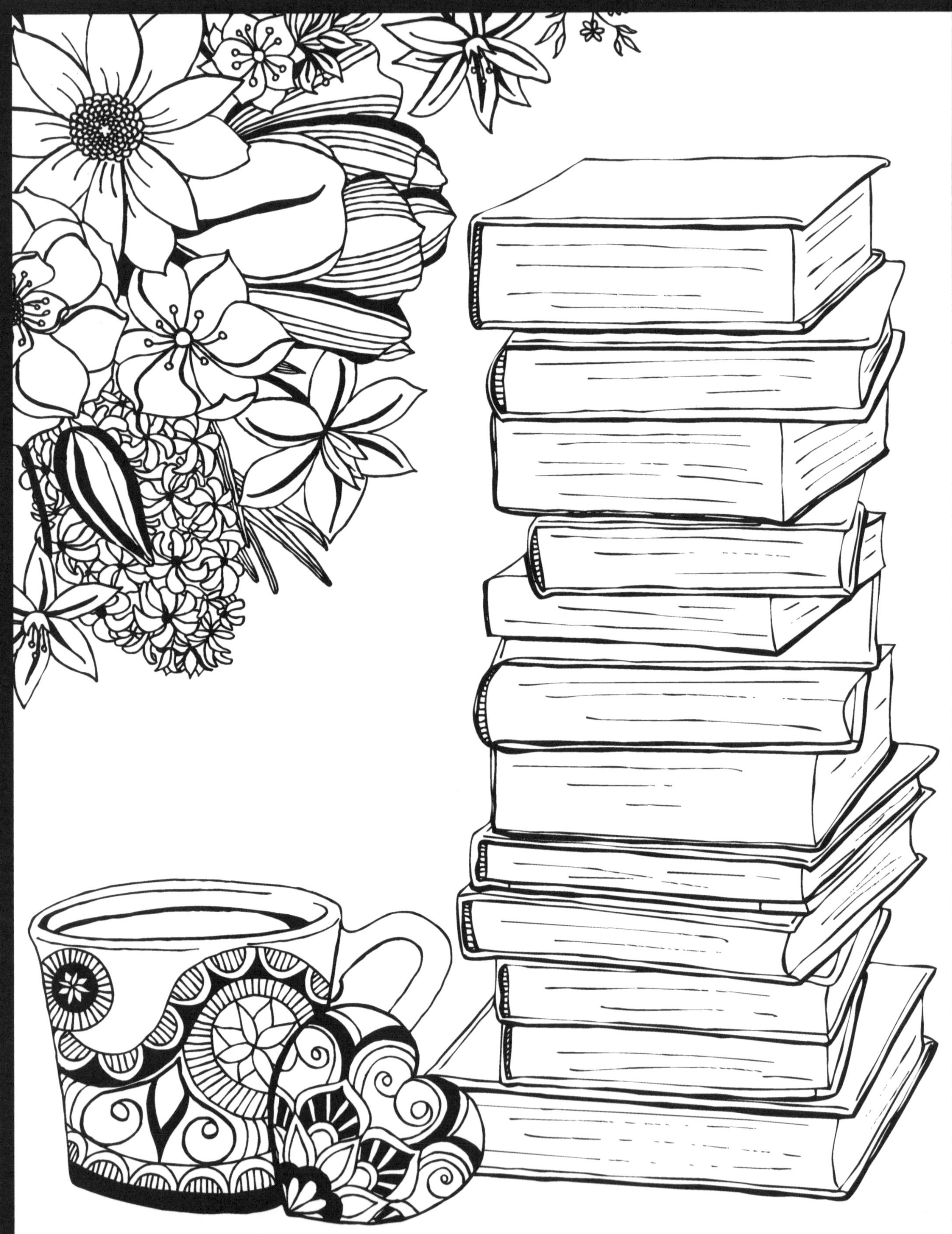

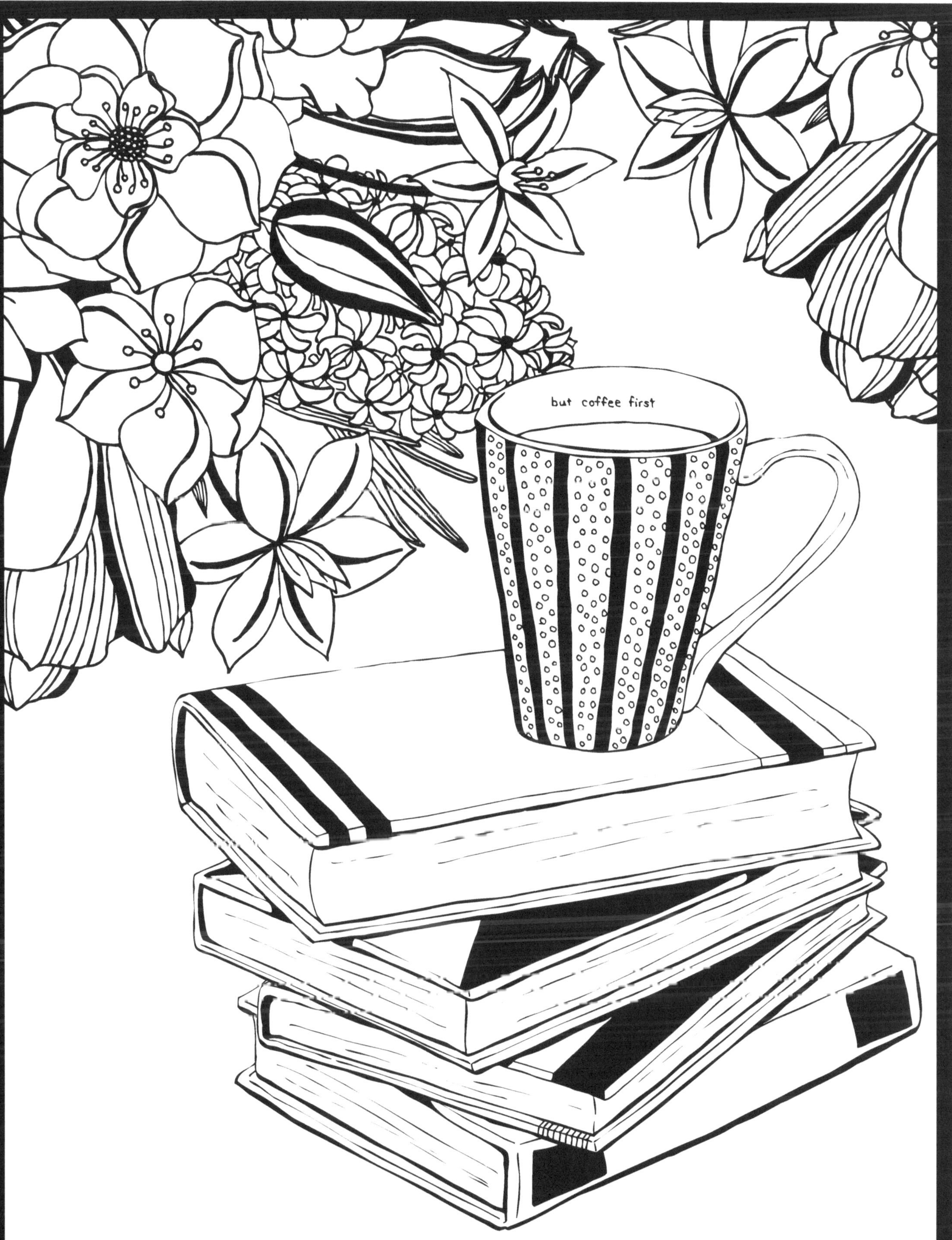
but coffee first